# Elements of Mindfulness

# Elements of Mindfulness

A Practical Guide to Cultivate *Goodness*, *Joy* and *Synergy* in Life

Prem Gopal Das

VY BOOKS

Vedanta Yogashala
1, Crooked Lane, Kolkata 700069
India.



P-ISBN: 978-81-965665-3-1
E-ISBN: 978-81-965665-8-6

E-mail: info@vedantayogashala.in
Web: www.vedantayogashala.in

*To all my students,*
*teaching you taught me life's*
*most valuable lessons*

Once you've finished reading, I would greatly appreciate it if you could take a moment to leave a sincere rating or review on Amazon. Your feedback helps others feel confident in choosing this book.

I wish you a fulfilling journey on the sublime path of Mindfulness!

For further clarification on the subject, feel free to write to me at premgopal@vedantayogashala.in

# *Contents*

# 1

# *Introduction*

## Unmindfully mindful

I lived as a monk in a monastery in downtown Kolkata, along with twenty other inmates.

One morning, while I was engrossed in work, a message alert on my mobile grabbed my attention. Rashmi sent out a plea to the messaging group we shared: *Everyone, please pray for Ankur. He is in the hospital with a brain stroke.*

*Which hospital?* I quickly messaged her.

She called back to explain that Ankur had had a brain stroke the night before and was admitted into the Institute of Neurosciences ICU. She sounded scared and broken.

"How is he doing right now?" I asked.

"His condition is critical. Though conscious, he seems to have lost his memory. He can't recognise anyone, not even family members. Sometimes he is hallucinating," she replied.

The hospital was close to my monastery, and I decided to visit Ankur. It was raining outside. I took an umbrella and walked my way. My mind was flooded with all the interactions I had had with Ankur. I met him and Rashmi four years back when their children joined the Value Education classes I coordinated.

I knew Ankur had been struggling with health issues for quite some time. It all started in June 2016. Ankur, Rashmi, and their two daughters had just returned from an overseas vacation, fond memories of the trip still fresh in their hearts. Eventually, school started for the children, Ankur got involved with his office, and Rashmi got busy with chores. The time seemed to pass happily. Little could anyone guess the danger lying ahead.

One evening, without any forewarning, Ankur felt his whole body becoming stiff, and his right side had a substantial loss of sensation. After an initial diagnosis by a general physician, Ankur was referred to a neurosurgeon, as the problem seemed to be nerve-related.

The journey henceforth was quite turbulent, both for Ankur as well as for Rashmi. After trying out a melange of doctors, diagnoses, and medications, he eventually began his treatment at NIMHANS, Bangalore. The case was critical and involved a lot of trial-and-error medications. Both husband and wife kept travelling between the hospital in Bangalore and their home in Kolkata. Sometimes, the visits would be short for regular check-ups; at other times, Ankur would be admitted for *days* together.

It went on like this until mid-December 2016. In the last week of the year, the condition severely deteriorated for Ankur. Aching and loss of sensation spread over other parts of his body also. He was again rushed to NIMHANS. A new diagnosis and a revised medication required him to stay in the hospital for prolonged periods—sometimes *even* one month at a stretch.

Rashmi accompanied him throughout. Remaining away from a big joint family, her children, kith, and kin was very tough for her. The spiritual practices she was rooted in greatly helped to keep her emotionally strong. These intermittent visits to the hospital went on for three years, and his condition had been improving slowly until this sudden massive stroke last night.

Soon, I reached the hospital. Rashmi burst into tears while talking to me. Never had I seen her break down like this in the last three years when Ankur steadily recovered. Something didn't feel right, *yet* I was hopeful. I intended to offer personal prayers for Ankur's recovery and counsel the family to remain stable during this challenging time.

When I entered the ICU, I found Ankur hallucinating that he was driving a car with no brakes and was screaming and shouting at an imaginary crowd, "Get on the sidewalk, please move; I might have an accident. Please move. *Why* don't you listen? *Everyone* move aside."

He was flailing his hands and legs agitatedly. Two male attendants held him down, trying to keep him on the bed.

The ICU monitor showed an increased heart rate, blood pressure, and an abnormal ECG graph. The attendants tried their best to convince Ankur to calm down, repeating that everything was all right. This was my first experience of watching someone whose mind created a virtual world around him, where he was taking an illusion to be reality. His mind had taken complete control of all his sensory organs—he was seeing and hearing things that did not exist!

Once the hallucination passed and he was stable, I approached him, greeting him with a smile.

As expected, he didn't seem to recognise me. I told him I had come to offer prayers for his quick recovery. Ankur kept staring at me without speaking. My words didn't seem to make any sense to him. There was still much restlessness evident in him. He was breathing heavily. Not sure when another hallucination might occur, I chanted some prayers at his bedside. It went on for a few minutes. Ankur seemed to be listening, though without responding, his head hung low.

After I finished, I asked if there was something else I could do for him. I did not expect him to respond. For some time, Ankur seemed lost in thought in silence, and then suddenly, he broke into sobs. As I held his hand, he began murmuring incoherently through his moans; his head still hung low. I had to try hard to understand the broken words he was uttering.

Haltingly, he spoke about an incident where he had scolded his daughter so much that she had burst into tears, shouting, "*Papa aap to aise hi ho* (Papa, you are always like this)." Tears streamed down his cheeks as he recalled the incident.

I listened to him without judging. I could feel the pain in his heart.

Ankur closed his eyes and folded his hands in *Namaskar* mudra. Still avoiding eye contact, he continued, "I keep offending people. I wish that even unknowingly, I never do something that hurts others."

Slowly, his tears and sobs subsided. After venting his bottled-up emotions, he seemed a little relieved.

The way Ankur was repenting and the way he was speaking words of wisdom were unexpected, given his current so-called abnormal state of mind. They were far from the ramblings of a hallucinating man. I realised this was nothing short of mindful repentance.

Before leaving, I said, "I pray you recover fast and return home soon." I was not sure whether he understood my words. Or whether he had even recognised my presence.

I took his leave and came to the lounge, where other family members waited for their turn to meet Ankur. I told Rashmi about my interaction with Ankur and asked whether Ankur had recently had a fallout with one of his daughters. She revealed that Ankur had severely scolded his elder daughter just two days before the stroke, and his daughter was so hurt that she had burst out in frustration, "*Papa aap to aise hi ho*"—the very words Ankur, even in his troubled state of mind, had not forgotten.

It was astonishing that in his current incoherent state when Ankur could not recognise even his family members, he could vividly recall this incident before the stroke. Not only did he remember the incident, but he also repented probably much more mindfully than others do in their so-called normal state of mind.

It took three weeks before Ankur could recognise anyone properly. After three months, he managed to walk. According to the doctors, it was unprecedented how Ankur survived such a severe attack and recovered so fast. The whole family took it as a blessing, the abundance of divine grace.

Once, I asked him, "Ankur, do you remember when I visited you in the ICU?"

He gave his usual sweet smile and replied, "*No.*"

This incident prompted me to dive a little deeper to understand our minds' subtle and complex functioning.

## What is Mindfulness?

The mind is the most influential part of our being, crucial for our overall physical and emotional health. The mind governs our senses and serves as the source and repository of our desires, thoughts, emotions & experiences.

As the saying goes, we are where our mind is. In general, our mind tends to focus on everything other than the activity at hand. The mind may get completely engrossed in overwhelming thoughts, making us utterly oblivious to our surroundings, including our body. It can host strong undercurrents of emotions—worries, fear, grudges, anxiety, tension, prejudices, uncertainty about the future—whose adverse effects can be seen on our health, in relationships, in terms of reduced efficiency at study or work, or our general day to day functioning.

Practising mindfulness and related techniques can provide us with valuable tools, using which, instead of living in a virtual bubble (created within the mind), we can bring the mind to a more effective state where our actions are the results of a series of conscious responses, rather than being the response generated by an unmindful state.

In its basic form, mindfulness is the art of bringing our awareness into the present by striking a balance between what we think, say, and mean and what we actually do. A broader aspect of mindfulness would also involve adding quality to whatever we do. E.g. a basic element of mindful eating would be to bring our awareness and attention fully into the act of consuming the food, whereas a broader aspect of it would involve the conscious selection of cooking ingredients and proper attention to the cooking process.

Similarly, mindful talking would involve not only paying attention to what we are saying but also being aware of how we are saying it and the intention behind the words, all while keeping the desired outcome in mind.

As the book progresses, chapter by chapter, we will explore how the concept of 'mindfulness' can have an all-pervading presence in our lives. It can be applied anytime, anywhere—while walking, driving, at work, at home, dealing with children and family members, studying, etc. There is always a scope for applying the principles of mindfulness in practically anything we do.

## Invest time mindfully

In the beginning, it does take conscious effort and a bit of your precious time to internalise the principles of mindfulness. Still, eventually, it comes naturally in how you choose to respond to any given situation mindfully. The investment of time in honing its practices is like sharpening a pencil. If the tip becomes dull, you need to take the time to sharpen the pencil to maintain writing with the same efficiency. Although it may require some extra time and effort, in the end, it not only saves you time but also enhances the quality of your writing.

Just like a pencil, our mind can also become worn out, fatigued, or 'drained out of its energy' from constantly processing thoughts, emotions, and interactions in our daily lives. That's why it's important to pause for a while to use an appropriate mindfulness tool to help refresh and rejuvenate the mind, thus bringing our consciousness to a more effective state.

One simple *yet* effective mindfulness tool is focusing our awareness on the act of breathing.

### ACTIVITY TIME

## Mindful breathing exercise

(Estimated practice time 4–5 Minutes)

Mindful breathing is an activity integrating our awareness into the physical act of breathing. Sit down either on a chair or cross-legged on the floor. Make yourself comfortable and practice deep breathing, focusing on the movements of inhaled and exhaled air. Feel the sensation of the inhaled air at the tip of your nose. Visualise and feel the inhaled air travelling through your windpipe to your lungs. Fill the lungs to the maximum capacity. Feel the vitality and the freshness that the inhaled air adds to your body and mind. Take a moment to thank Mother Nature for supplying you with this life-giving force. Hold your breath for a few seconds before gently releasing it.

Breathe in again, repeating the same process. As you inhale this time, try to feel that a part of the inhaled air also goes into your belly, causing it to fill and shrink with every breath. Continue conscious breathing at your normal pace, ensuring you remain relaxed. See if you can feel the temperature of the air as it enters and exits your body, noting that the inhaled air is cool while the exhaled air is relatively warm.

The sequence of mindful breathing is as follows:

1. Inhale slowly, focusing on your breath
2. Gently hold your breath for some time
3. Exhale slowly
4. Gently hold your breath for some time before the next inhalation
5. Inhale again, repeating the same process while keeping your attention on the internal path of the inhaled air.

Practice deep inhaling and exhaling 12–15 times or more, depending on your comfort. The whole exercise should be smooth. Don't rush to finish the task at hand. Eyes can either be closed or open as you feel comfortable.

Taking a few conscious deep breaths has the immense potential to calm the mind by bringing our awareness to the present. It also gives clarity of thought and action. The gentle inhalation and exhalation sustain us, comfort us, affect our thoughts, and preserve our harmony.

*However*, there can be certain impediments to the process. Often, in the beginning, or even in the later stages of mindfulness practice, a thought can beset us, 'When will this exercise be over so that I am free to do what I like to or have to do?' While going through the breathing exercise, our mind is bound to get swayed by similar distracting thoughts. Don't judge yourself if this happens. This is quite natural, and this is how the mind functions for all of us.

Whenever this happens, or instead when you realise that the mind has drifted, gently redirect your focus to your breathing. It is often difficult to trace what led the mind to wander, but see if you can discover what was in your mind when you realised it had strayed.

The simplicity of mindful breathing exercise is that it does not necessarily require a formal setup. One can do it at any time and place that suits them, whether it be at home, while walking, at work, while studying, cooking, or even lying down in bed. And as a natural consequence, one will achieve a state that makes them emotionally happier and, thus, physically healthier.

# 2

# *The Working Principle Behind Mindfulness*

## Default object of meditation

The current focus of your thoughts can be considered your mind's 'default object of meditation' at this moment. It can change multiple times within a short span of time. The 'default object of meditation' can be versatile—It may consist of troubling thoughts, a strong yearning, cherished memories, or exciting prospects for the future. The range of thoughts that may pop up on the surface of the mind at any given moment is as unpredictable as limitless.

## Chosen object of meditation

Your 'chosen object of meditation' is the object, activity, or thought you consciously chose to focus on. During a mindful breathing exercise, conscious awareness about the 'act of breathing' itself is your 'chosen object of meditation'. Few conscious breathings enable the mind to make a transition from its 'default object of meditation' (consisting of unpredictable random thoughts) to your 'chosen object of meditation' (which in this case is focusing on the act of breathing, Fig. 2.1).

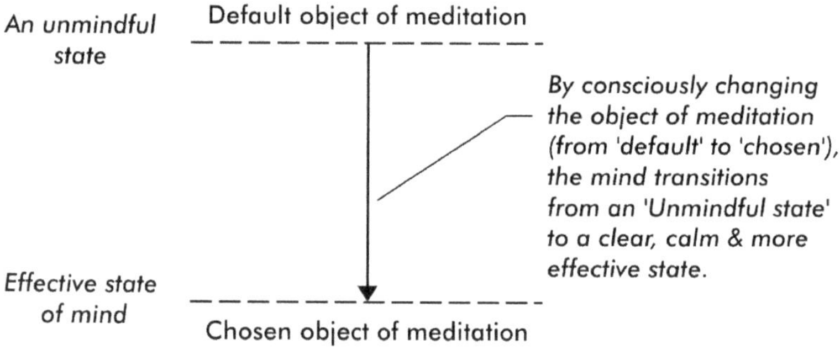


Fig. 2.1

And in doing so, instead of allowing it to get drained out of its energy, the mind is streamlined to achieve a more calm, clear, and effective state—which indeed is the purpose of mindfulness.

Even while practising mindful breathing exercise, the thoughts within the mind may keep oscillating between its 'chosen' and 'default' object of meditation (Fig. 2.2). Through

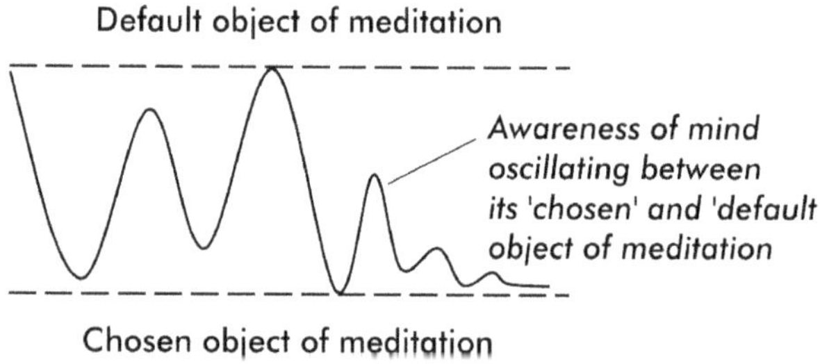


Fig. 2.2

consistent practice, one can train the mind to remain more focused on the chosen object of meditation.

Your chosen object of meditation may not necessarily be 'mindful breathing'. You have the freedom to direct your focus towards anything that can help you be more mindful and present, whether it be your posture, your steps, a mantra, or the beauty of your surroundings—in short, anything that resonates with you and engages your attention in a meaningful way.

## Applying mindfulness to manage anger

The feeling of anger is a strong urge inside us, which, when channelled properly, has its own use in life. However, the problem arises when the outburst of anger becomes disproportionate or uncontrolled. That means instead of being able to regulate it, anger takes control over our thoughts and actions.

Often outbursts of anger could surface as an outcome of one or more of the ongoing preceding negative emotions inside us, such as grudges, frustration, envy, stress, neglect, etc. Anger is a highly noticeable emotion, unlike the silent symptoms of emotions that lead to anger.

Expressing anger harshly can lead to a series of unmindful actions regarding speech and/or physical harm to property and people around us. On the other hand, keeping anger bottled up within us can cause serious psychological and physical damage. Therefore, learning how to channel this volatile emotion carefully is necessary.

## Analysing a generic case of anger

Various interactions throughout the day might lead to different degrees of frustration, grudges, and a buried form of anger inside a person. In the evening, when they return home, they may 'blow off' all or some of these buried emotions in the form of anger outbursts on their family members. What this outburst requires is, maybe, just a small stimulus or trigger (Fig. 2.3).

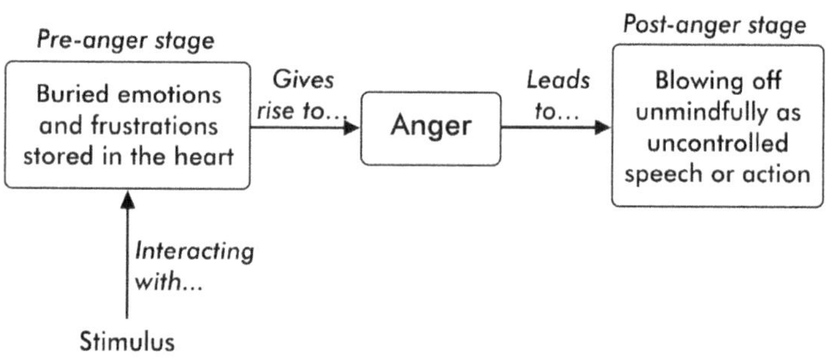


*Fig. 2.3*

At what point a person 'blows off' will depend on that individual's tolerance level.

## A mindful solution

### *Pre-anger management*

Be mindful of the rise of anger in your heart. This is the awareness part of mindfulness. Identify the things or situations which have the potential to trigger your anger. The next stage would be to do everything possible to avoid these and eliminate or minimise trigger situations.

Taking a few mindful breaths at certain intervals during the day can act as a set of small relief valves that intermittently release the built-up pressure of buried emotions inside the mind (Fig. 2.4) before it blows off in a big and nasty way.

Any stimulus, in this case, will interact now with a relatively more effective state of mind, leading to a controlled and more manageable form of anger, which can be addressed more meaningfully.

### *Post-anger management*

Whenever some stimulus provokes you towards an outburst of anger, you need to create a time lag between the surfacing of your anger and your response to it. This time lag is termed as Pause Action (Fig. 2.4).

For instance, when you get angry next time, count from 1 to 10 in your mind or take a few deep breaths as your Pause Action. In essence, by inserting a Pause Action, you are shifting the mind's focus from its default object of meditation (in this case, on the cause of anger) to its chosen object of meditation (the activity you chose for your Pause Action). Doing so allows the turbulence in your mind to settle, reaching an effective state of mind where you can respond thoughtfully to vent anger.

Achieving this may seem challenging at first, but with consistent and conscious effort, it is indeed possible to swiftly insert a 'Pause Action' between a fast-acting stimulus and your response to it.

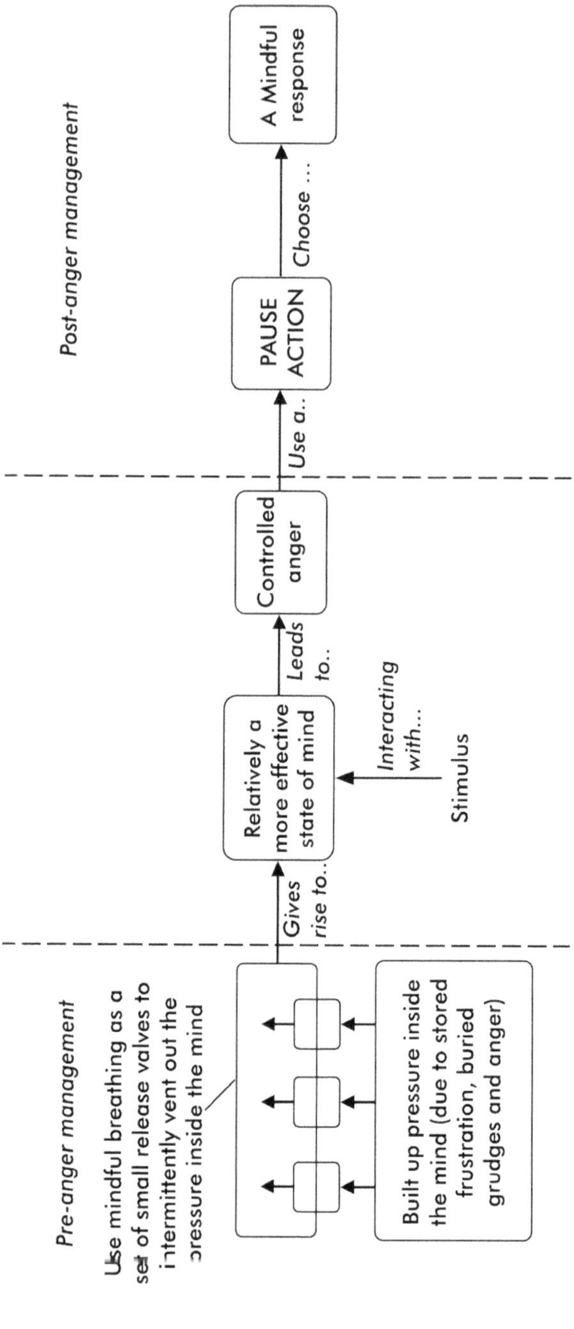


*Fig. 2.4. Solution for a stimulus based anger — A mindful approach*

Can you think of two alternative ways to effectively use as a Pause Action to control your anger the next time you feel pulled towards it?

________________________ ________________________

## Intention matters

"How can I manage my anger?" Manisha once asked me.

I was somewhat aware of the strained relationship she was going through with Ishaan, her 14-year-old son, who happened to be part of my Teen Empowerment class.

Whenever her son disobeyed or differed from her, Manisha would find herself helplessly dragged into a state where she would invariably vent her anger out on Ishaan, often in disproportionate ways, which she would regret later once the anger passed.

"All the good advice is not of much use," I told Manisha, "if your child's heart is closed to take any instruction. One of the things that a teenager hates most is nagging. It creates an invisible wall between you and them. You may have a good reason for correcting or even being angry with him, but doing so at this point in time will distance you further from him. First, gain your son's trust by bringing back the warmth of a mutual relationship."

I took some time to explain to her the concept of pre- and post-anger management. The Pause Action I suggested to her was—*Let go of small things.* "Avoid bringing conflict over trivial and small issues," I told her.

After a few weeks, I happened to meet her again. I was curious to know if she could apply the principle I had suggested.

"I am facing a new problem now," she said, "My son doubts my intention. I have been able to control my anger for a few days at a stretch using the letting go technique you taught me by letting go of small differences that would create a deep divide between us. But there are moments after a few days when eventually I lose my temper and burst out, venting all my anger on my son. And my son responds, "Mom, this is what your real nature is. All that peaceful gesture of the last few days was just a *show-off!*" And it tears my heart to hear this," Manisha sighed.

It is indeed immensely painful when your right intentions are doubted. Giving selfless love is not easy, and being suspected of our intention is often an integral part of it. However, as I told her, one should keep persisting and improving. Failure is not a failure as long as it's a stepping stone to success. Understanding this and remembering it is important, especially when confronting challenging situations.

Changing our inner nature is not an overnight activity. The goal of using a Pause Action is not to make us perfect but rather to bring us closer to something more acceptable. And this journey takes time and patience. It took a few months for Manisha's relationship with Ishaan to improve considerably.

Though there are still some moments of conflict, the frequency has reduced a lot. All it took from Manisha was to persistently work on using her 'Pause Action' efficiently. For her, the Pause Action was 'letting go of small differences' with her son.

## Complex cases of anger

Sometimes, anger can become so ingrained in a person that it becomes their default emotion. They may experience anger without any external triggers. How mindfulness practices can attempt to change the nature of a person in such situations will be discussed in later chapters.

### ACTIVITY TIME

Can you recall any incident where you became disproportionately angry with someone and did or said something you wish you hadn't? (Take a moment to pause and reflect on the incident).

What was the incident?

________________________________________

________________________________________

Can you recall the cause of your anger?

________________________________________

Was there any time lag between the surfacing of anger and your response to it?

________________________________________

Could you have conveyed your anger in a more meaningful way?

________________________________________

________________________________________

________________________________________

________________________________________

________________________________________

# 3

# *Perception Matters*

## Gross body

Our gross body refers to the physical aspect of ourselves that can be easily perceived through touch and sight. Although we perceive it as composed of flesh and bones, it ultimately consists of the five elements: earth, water, fire, air, and ether.

The solid constituents of our body fall under the category of earth. When we break it down, the components of bones, flesh, and muscle consist mostly of earth and water. Our blood contains almost ninety per cent of water. Then there are fluids around the heart, lungs, abdomen, brain, in intestine, all having water as a major component. As vapour, water is also present in all segments of airways and different segments of food pipes. On a micro level, water is also present inside the cells as space fluid. With sixty per cent of our body weight, water is the most prominent constituent of our gross body.

Air is found mainly in the lungs and in other areas, such as the throat, stomach, intestines, rectum and anus. The gross body also contains air in dissolved form in the blood and in ionic form in tissue fluids. The fire part is what aids body mechanisms like digestion and helps in keeping the body warm. Ether refers to the physical space our body occupies, which naturally changes as a child grows.

Thus, earth, water, fire, air and ether, in combination with one another, give rise to our gross body, a vehicle for action.

## Working of the senses

Eyes, tongue, ears, skin and nose are the five 'knowledge acquiring senses' (*gyanendriya*), which respectively give us information about the form, taste, sound, touch and aroma of things around us. These five senses are the only gateways through which we can perceive anything in this world. Collectively, form, taste, sound, touch and smell are called sense objects, i.e. these are the 'objects of perception' by their corresponding knowledge-acquiring senses. The Vedic texts refer to sense objects as *rupa* (form), *rasa* (taste), *shabda* (sound), *sparsh* (touch), and *gandha* (smell).

Each knowledge-acquiring sense organ has a specific limitation—it can only perceive its corresponding sense object. E.g., our eyes can provide us with details about the appearance, such as colour and shape, of a specific dish but cannot offer any insights into its taste or aroma. The nose can detect the smell of food but offers no insight into its flavour or visual appearance. Although the ears can provide information about a person's voice, they cannot indicate the speaker's appearance.

Interestingly, some of our knowledge-acquiring senses combine seamlessly to give us a total sensation. For instance, the tongue allows us to perceive the food's flavour and determine its temperature, whether hot or cold. This is because the tongue's skin collaborates with its taste buds, providing us with dual sensory information.

## The function of the mind

The information gathered by all the 'knowledge-acquiring senses' is transmitted to the mind. Our sense organs cannot directly experience any object on their own (Fig. 3.1). Their

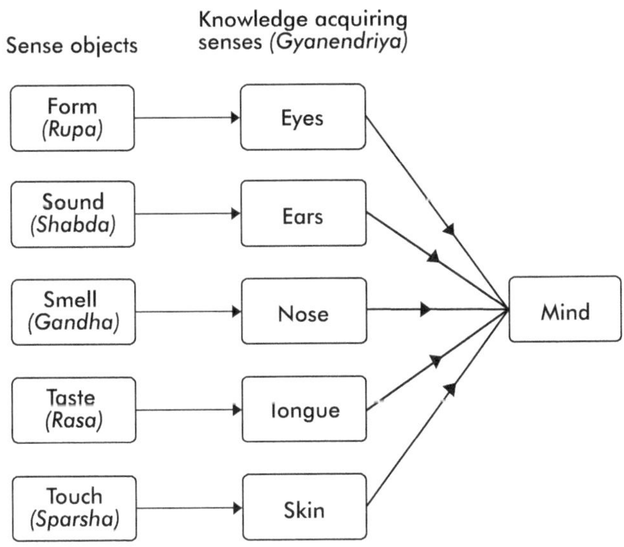


Fig. 3.1

function is just to collect sensory data. For example, our eyes function similarly to a camera; they gather data on the appearance and shape of objects and transmit it to the mind. The perception of sight is generated within the mind rather than the eyes themselves.

In the same way, the perception of smell, sound, taste, and touch is generated in the mind rather than in the corresponding sensory organs. Our mind serves as a repository of past impressions and information while acting as the epicentre for developing new experiences and emotions. Hankering, lamentation, accepting and rejecting an idea, aversion, and attachments are some of the default settings of the mind, among innumerable others.

When we say 'mind', we're referring here not to the brain, which is an intricately complex organ inside our skull made up of various neural tissues. Instead, we're referring to a more subtle aspect of our being that cannot be seen or touched through our physical senses. The brain is a part of our gross body, while the mind is subtle. The mind can be perceived through its functions of thinking, feeling and willing.

The brain acts as a crucial intermediary, facilitating communication between the senses responsible for acquiring knowledge and the mind, allowing signals to be transmitted in both directions. Our emotions, feelings, and experiences originate in the mind and are conveyed to the physical body through the brain. The brain, sometimes also referred to as the gross mind, is considered a subset of the subtle mind. The functioning of the mind can be likened to software, which is the actual operating principle behind the brain's hardware.

The mind is referred to in Sanskrit as '*manas*', a term commonly used whenever practices like yoga and meditation are discussed. Unless otherwise stated, wherever we use the term 'mind' in this book, we refer to '*manas*', the subtle aspect of our body.

## Aversion and attachment

Our mind forms perceptions towards any sense objects based on countless interactions with the world around us. For instance, you may feel happy if someone offers you ice cream. It's possible that you are drawn to that specific ice cream flavour because your memory associates it with a positive experience in the past. The mere thought of getting another chance to taste it brings happiness, even before experiencing the flavour.

Conversely, an individual who doesn't have a craving for ice cream will feel unaffected by it, even if presented with the same ice cream.

Whether we crave, feel indifferent towards, or dislike ice cream (or anything else) is not determined by the object itself but rather by how our minds perceive it.

## Further analysis of sense objects

In certain scenarios, multiple senses can contribute to accurately perceiving an object's true characteristics. An example of experiencing ice cream involves using multiple senses. One can touch the coldness, see its form, smell it, or hear the street vendor shouting loudly, '*Iiiice* Cream'. However, the tongue is the primary sense that perceives the taste of the ice cream. When watching a movie, our primary senses involved are sight and sound. Other senses may need to be more engaged. To check the temperature of hot water, you can use your sense of touch. Nevertheless, you can also rely on other senses. For instance, if you observe the water boiling, you wouldn't need to touch it to know its temperature.

## Varieties within the sense objects

The mind solely processes input through the five senses, and within each sense lies an extensive range of diversity. Consider the six basic tastes: sweet (*madhur*), sour (*amla*), salty (*lavana*), pungent (*katu*), bitter (*tikta*), and astringent (*kashaya*). The combination and proportion of six basic tastes results in countless variations in the flavour of different foods and beverages, each with its distinct taste.

When we hear a sound, we can infer the presence of a speaker or a sound source. Various sounds can possess different attributes, such as loud, screeching, soft, melodious, rough, or cacophonous. Touch can evoke a range of sensations, such as roughness, hardness, temperature, slipperiness, stickiness, and more. Itching is a distinct sensation that can be felt on the skin. In fact, for the skin, the object of perception is touch, while the hair on the skin gives rise to the perception of itching.

Strong, soft, fragrant and foul are some of the varieties of smells. When you incorporate spices into your cooking, the resulting smell becomes a blend of various scents.

You don't need physical contact between your senses and their corresponding objects to perceive form, smell, or sound. For example, your eyes don't physically touch the object they observe. Similarly, ears can pick up distant thunder, and the nose can detect far-off scents. However, the tongue and skin can only perceive objects when brought into proximity or direct contact.

In addition to our senses for acquiring knowledge, our bodies also have active working senses such as the mouth, hands, legs, anus, genital, etc. These senses facilitate the active working of the body. They function according to the dictates of the mind, being assisted in their work by knowledge-acquiring senses.

Interestingly, the mouth has multiple functions. As a knowledge-acquiring sense, the mouth (the tongue in it) gives information about taste; simultaneously, as a working sense, the mouth has the function of chewing and speaking. So, in all, the mouth has three functions—tasting, chewing and speaking.

## A mindful perception

Once, I was travelling by a local train from Kolkata en route to Krishna Nagar, a traditional ancient town in the Nadia district of West Bengal. The city also is a gateway to many places of spiritual significance located in the vicinity.

As the train departed from the station, several vendors entered the compartment where I was seated to sell their merchandise, as was usual. If you happen to take a local train in this part of India, you'll experience a vibrant marketplace on wheels. Vendors present a diverse array of products, including hand-woven towels and handkerchiefs, toys, keychains, purses, herbal medicines, toothpaste, fruits, sweets, and savoury treats—to name a few.

I was lucky enough to manage a coveted window seat. As the train pulled into the lush green countryside, I was captivated by the panoramic view unfolding before me.

Soon enough, my attention was captured by a beautiful melody sung by a young couple who likely boarded the train at the previous station. They accompanied their singing with humble musical instruments, performing traditional folk songs. Previously, I had encountered singers who performed a few songs on a moving train and then requested money for their livelihood. However, this particular instance was unique as both the husband and wife were visually impaired.

However, their physical blindness didn't seem to be much of an obstacle in their work. They were slowly and surely moving inside the compartment, singing and requesting donations from every person. *Certainly*, it was a struggle for them to commute daily in local trains, which are usually crowded for a large portion of the day. However, their demeanour exuded contentment. True joy is a symptom of the heart that naturally reflects on a person's face.

The woman was dressed modestly in a sari with her head covered. Her wheatish complexion complemented her beauty. Ironically, her eyes couldn't reveal this truth to her. In general, people in this world get mesmerised by the external beauty of the body, which only goes skin deep. However, neither the woman nor her husband subscribed to this shallow notion of beauty. Seeing is a process of perceiving the world around us, but it can also be done, probably more meaningfully, through senses other than our eyes.

For this couple, the lack of reliance on their physical eyes led them to develop a deeper and more meaningful way of perceiving the world around them. They seemed to be very mindful of every interaction they had between themselves and others.

As they disembarked at the next station, a revelation occurred to me:

*Certainly, the senses help us to collect information about the world around us, but how our mind perceives those sensory inputs will very much depend on what virtues we hold valuable.*

# 4

# *The Mind-Body Connections*

## Interfunctioning of senses, mind, and intelligence

Imagine this scenario: It's Sunday morning, and you're headed to the market to purchase some vegetables. As you make your way through the bustling marketplace, a *delightful* aroma catches your attention. Here's what could happen next.

### 1:

The mind naturally seeks to identify the source of the smell; the mind will signal the brain to turn the neck and adjust the eyes to get a better view of the surrounding area to look for all the probable causes for this smell.

You see the source of the smell to be your favourite sweet, hot *jalebis*[*], being fried at a nearby sweetshop. You might have had an earlier good experience of tasting hot *jalebis* at this

[*] A traditional Indian sweet made of batter, deep fried, and steeped in sugar syrup.

shop, and your mind brings up that memory. By now, your mind has already developed a hankering to enjoy the taste of the hot *jalebi*. This might even make your mouth water!

### 2:

The mind is filled with the desire to eat the *jalebis,* so it sends a signal to the brain, causing the legs to walk towards the sweetshop while your eyes watch the skilled *halwai* (the sweet maker) sitting outside the shop in front of a stove, applying his expertise in giving shape to the batter which is getting fried in *ghee*, in a black colour iron frying pan, creating a satisfying, crisp sound, emanating irresistible aroma.

For the time being, you forget everything else in the world as your mind becomes consumed with the longing to savour the delicious taste of *jalebi.*

### 3:

By now, your mind has become adamant about making a halt by the sweet shop to eat the *Jalebis*. Your intelligence, which was dormant in the background, comes into action now.

The mind tends to go by its instinct; however, intelligence is our discriminating power, which like a wise person, guides us to make an appropriate choice in every situation. As a decision maker, intelligence (known in Sanskrit as *buddhi*) is considered even subtler than the mind. A conversation begins now between your mind and intelligence (Fig. 4.1).

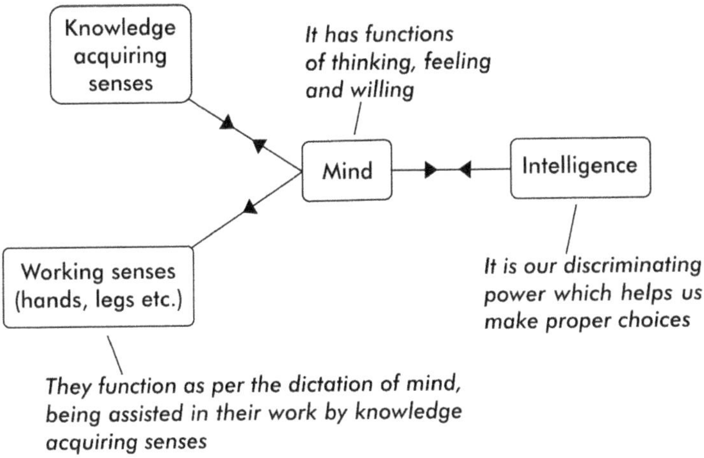


Fig. 4.1

Intelligence may advise the mind, "*No*. You already have diabetes. Don't eat *Jalebi*. Can't you recall how much you suffered last time after eating *Jalebis?*" But the mind may deceive the intelligence by rationalising, "Just two pieces of it; after all, how often do I get the fortune of enjoying hot *Jalebis?*"

In this tussle between mind and intelligence, who will win depends on who is stronger of the two. Ideally, the mind is supposed to be guided by a clear intellect, but when intelligence becomes weak, the mind overpowers it.

**4:**

If your mind wins, you will enter the sweetshop and end up eating the *jalebis*.

But usually, the desire for more *Jalebis* persists. Your tongue likes the taste so much that it craves the delectable flavour and wants to eat a few more *Jalebis*. The intelligence which was engaged in an ongoing tussle with the mind again takes charge, forbidding your mind from sending any more signals to indulge in additional *Jalebis*.

Assuming your intelligence prevails this time, the mind will command the brain to signal the hands to take out the money and settle the bill. Subsequently, the legs will be instructed to depart the shop and continue walking towards the vegetable market, your intended destination.

The series of interactions between the senses, mind, and intelligence happens at such a rapid pace that it gives us the feeling that the whole thing is happening instantaneously. *However*, if observed minutely, you will find that the entire working process involves a step-by-step interaction between senses (*Gyanendriya* and *karmendriya*), mind, and intelligence. It is like piercing a closed lotus using a needle. While it may seem that all the petals are stuck at once, but in effect, petals are pierced one by one, one after another.

## An incident in a Gurukul

This story is from a Gurukul, a traditional Vedic school nestled in picturesque countryside. Boys would be sent there to spend many years as full-time boarding students to learn under a Guru, the master, who would guide and instruct them. Their training began from a very early age in material, social and spiritual knowledge, along with martial arts.

Once, the Guru selected a small vacant room in the Gurukul and assigned a student each day to fill up this room to the maximum extent possible with something meaningful. The condition was that the students could purchase anything within one hundred rupees, which the Guru gave to them on each subsequent day.

On the first day, the chosen student acquired several baskets filled with cheap, aged vegetable stock. The stock took up nearly a quarter of the room's space. Another student ventured to a nearby village the following day, searching for a cost-effective yet valuable commodity. He came across a farmer threshing rice from paddy. The student bargained for the price of the husk and managed to purchase a substantial amount for just a hundred rupees. He could fill half the room with it. On the third day, a different student was selected. He promptly returned after just half an hour and handed over ninety-seven rupees to the Guru. The student exclaimed, "Gurudev, I have filled the entire room with just 3 rupees."

The Guru went to inspect the student's purchase of 3 rupees that supposedly filled the entire room. He discovered only a candle and an incense stick burning in the room.

The student meekly clarified, "Gurudev, I bought a candle, an incense stick, and a matchbox, each for one rupee. The light of the candle and the fragrance of the burning incense stick filled the entire room."

The Guru was happy. He called all the students in the Gurukul and explained, "This room represents our mind, and what we fill it with is more important than how much we fill it. When the input to the mind is pure, what follows is pure thoughts and pure actions."

All the students sat around the Guru, who was seated on an elevated platform as he continued explaining, "Observing Nature, we see moths that helplessly succumb to the attraction of a light source, such as a burning lamp. They emerge en masse during the evening, only to meet their demise by morning from falling into fires or the flames of lamps. The strong hankering of their eyes to enjoy the effulgence of the flame proves to be the cause of their destruction.

"Then there is the example of bees. They buzz around fragrant flowers, getting captivated by the smell. Some of them enter deep inside the flower, and as evening approaches, the bee fails to realise that the flower petals are closing. As a result, they get entrapped inside the closed petals and suffocate. The next day morning, the flower petals may reopen, but the bee is already dead by then. Normally, a bee is strong enough to pierce through the soft layers of petals. But the sweet nectar emanating from the flower makes the bee so intoxicated that they lose both intelligence and strength to make any attempt to come out of the entrapment.

"Fishes' insatiable yearning to sample different things is widely known," the Guru said. "Despite having access to many food sources in river water, their overwhelming craving to try everything drives them to nibble on fishermen's bait. Consequently, they end up getting caught, and this weakness for a taste ultimately leads to their demise.

"Wild deer suffer because of their susceptibility to sound. In the past, some skilled hunters would lure these animals with a specific melody played on the flute. This would bring the deer within reach of the hunter, making it simple to capture them.

"Finally, there is the example of elephants. One of the traditional ways of capturing a male elephant in the forest is to bring a trained female elephant in view of the male elephant. The male elephant charges towards her, anticipating the happiness of touch, the culmination of which is sexual enjoyment. There is a ditch made beforehand on the path of the male elephant. The female elephant is trained to go around this ditch, but the male elephant runs straight and falls into the ditch, cushioned inside and covered at the top with a bunch of leaves. This allows for his eventual capture and subsequent training in load-carrying services."

The students listened intently, at times looking toward the Guru and at other times toward the lit candle and aromatic incense stick.

"Let me *summarise,*" said the Guru.

"The moth's excessive attraction to form, the bee's attraction to smell, the fish's attraction to taste, the deer's attraction to sound, and the elephant's attraction to touch all lead to their destruction. As human beings, all five of our senses are fully developed. Then, how can a person who engages all his senses unrestrictedly in the five sense objects not be destroyed?

"So, for us, it becomes all the more important to learn how to check the undue demands of the senses, otherwise; as a strong wind sweeps away a boat on the water, even one of the roaming senses on which the mind focuses in a wrong way can carry away a person's intelligence.

"Our eyes irresistibly drag us towards something beautiful, ears want to hear something nice, the nose wants to smell something pleasant, and skin wants to touch or feel something soft. But amongst all, the tongue is the most difficult to control. It has a strong inclination to eat or drink something delicious. Moreover, the tongue also has a strong urge to talk."

"The demands of the senses are not to be denied," the Guru emphasised, "but I am talking about learning the importance of not engaging the senses in a way that is not appropriate. It is imperative that individuals cultivate a lifestyle centred around positive habits when it comes to their eating, sleeping, communication, leisure, and other daily routines. The initial step should be to establish an unwavering resolve and monitor the irrational urges of the senses, not through deprivation, but by providing them with purposeful engagement."

To enhance experiential learning, the Guru posed the question, "Who here knows how to fly a kite?"

Nearly all participants responded with an affirmative hand raise.

The Guru shared his childhood memories, "When I was your age, we would spend significant time in the Gurukul flying kites, especially during autumn when there is a good gust of wind. We made our own big kites. It was a little time-consuming but worth it. We felt very accomplished when the kite would soar high in the sky. Sometimes we engaged in matches, too. We would glue fine glass particles onto the kite string and "attack" other kites in the sky by swooping on the string of another kite and tugging at it with ours till the string of one of the kites would be severed. As soon as a kite flew off with a broken string, all of us would run behind the falling kite as far as possible, though mostly unsuccessful in our attempts to catch it."

The students beamed with delight as they listened to their Guru recall his childhood pastimes.

"The kite experiences stress in the string during normal flying conditions," the Guru continued. "This stress causes a downward force on the kite, which pulls it down. How many of you think this force limits the kite's ability to ascend higher in the sky?"

The boys were divided in their opinions. Some agreed while others were against it, though there appeared to be a lack of clarity regarding their stances. As the commotion subsided, the Guru began explaining again, "If you observe mindfully, you will find that it is the regulation of the string, this downward pulling force, which is helping the kite to soar high in the sky. This downward force gives a perfect angle for the kite to remain suspended high in the sky against the flow of the wind. As soon as the string is severed, the kite will land on the ground sooner or later."

All students gave their agreement with a nod of their heads.

Finally, the Guru added, "Our life situation is very similar to that of the kite. If we want ourselves to soar high in the sky of happiness, we need to keep ourselves under the control of the regulating string. A wise person is adept at engaging their senses of seeing, hearing, tasting, smelling, and touching, and thus, exercises a sense control known as the regulative principle of freedom. It frees you from the slavery of the senses. Only an individual who masters this art qualifies to become a perfect leader."

Saying this, the Guru concluded his lesson for the day, and the students *marvelled* at the fine life lessons explained to them through examples that they could easily relate to.

# 5

# *Consciousness*

## The concept of 'I'-ness

I was hurrying up for my scheduled class at National School. The school had invited me to take a series of eight lessons on Mindfulness. It was a weekly session to be delivered in the common assembly for class six students. Today was the fourth session in the series.

Before leaving the monastery, I did a quick inventory of my bag to ensure everything I needed was in place—printouts, pen, paper. With the bag in tow, I made my way out. The school was a bit of hike. I needed to arrive by ten a.m.

Children in this age group have always remained my favourite students. Throughout my experience teaching children for more than one and half decades, I found the age group of around 10–12 years to be the best time to inculcate some profound life lessons in them. You need to make learning engaging and enjoyable. They are at the perfect stage, being old enough to comprehend everything taught while still retaining their natural innocence, which is vital for learning.

When I reached the school, the boys and girls were still settling down on mats spread out in the assembly hall. They were familiar to me because of my previous interactions with them. There were around 60 students. My allotted slot was for 50 minutes.

I began by guiding a short mindful breathing practice, which I find quite effective in helping my audience cultivate a more receptive mindset. Following this, I inquired whether they had completed the previous assignment—writing a 'Thank You' note expressing their gratitude to all the people and things that mattered to them. Roughly half of them raised their hands in affirmation while I encouraged others to do the same.

With this, I moved on to the day's topic—the concept of 'I' ness.

I gave a set of instructions for the children to follow attentively. I started by asking them to point to their nose with their right hand. They followed with ease. Next, they were instructed to point to their ears, eyes, mouth, face, legs, and other limbs. Everyone easily followed the simple instructions. Then, I instructed them to point toward themselves. After a bit of deliberation, a few gestured towards their chest, others towards their stomach, face, etc.

"Which part of the body are *you* all pointing to?" I asked. Their replies indicated they were pointing to the 'body' as a whole.

I requested a volunteer to demonstrate a task. Among the handful who raised their hands, I chose a boy to come in front.

I asked his name. "Tanish," he replied.

"*Well*. Tanish, hear my instructions carefully and demonstrate them to all." As the students looked on, I took hold of Tanish's right hand and asked, "Tanish, whose hand is this?"

"*My* hand," he responded with ease.

"*Very good!*" Directing his attention to his nose, I followed up with Tanish, "To whom does this nose belong?"

As anticipated, he replied, "It's *me*."

I asked similar questions to Tanish about various aspects of his physicality, and he offered identical responses each time. Then directing his attention to his body, I asked, "Tanish, whose body is this?"

"It is *my* body," he replied spontaneously.

I then asked the final question in the series, "Tanish, who is the 'I' that claims ownership of this body?" This particular query seemed to perplex him, as he appeared uncertain of its meaning. The onlookers present displayed interest as I had successfully piqued their curiosity.

I displayed my marker pen to the group before writing the phrase "THIS IS MY PEN" on the board.

I then proceeded to explain the implications of this statement, jotting down four points for clarity's sake:

1. 'I' am different.
2. My pen is different.
3. 'I' have an identity separate from my pen.
4. 'I' have a choice, how I want to deal with this pen.

"My pen and 'I' myself are two different things," I emphasised. Continuing, I spoke, "Just like a person sitting inside a car—they are not the car itself, but rather a separate entity choosing to utilise the vehicle. In the same way, when someone declares, 'This is my house,' it means that they own the property, but they and the house are separate things. Similarly, 'I' myself, claiming to be the proprietor of this pen, has an identity separate from the pen, with the freedom to choose whether or not to use this pen."

Tanish remained at my side as I requested him to approach the whiteboard. I asked him to erase all instances of the word 'pen' and replace it with 'body'.

The new sentences conveyed the following meaning:

THIS IS MY BODY

It means

1. 'I' am different.
2. My body is different.
3. 'I' have an identity separate from my body.
4. 'I' have a choice, how I want to deal with this body.

I got the students to read out each of the above statements loud. Turning to Tanish, I asked him, "Given the discussion till now, can we *not* conclude that my body and 'I' myself, claiming to be the proprietor of the body, are two different entities?"

He contemplated for a while, then nodded in agreement. I thanked Tanish for his assistance and told him to return to his seat.

I continued to explain to everyone, "Situated as a tiny spark of energy, within the core of the heart, is our real self, this 'I', also commonly termed as 'soul'. It is responsible for keeping us alive by spreading consciousness throughout our body.

"Every moment, the cells in our body are constantly regenerated, and every seven years, our body is revamped by a whole set of newer cells. When we were babies, our bodies differed from what they are now. As we grow and go through youth, adulthood, and old age, our bodies constantly change. But despite such perpetual changes in the body, our real self, the 'I', the source of consciousness of the body, remains unchanged. Some people might lose their hands or legs in unfortunate accidents. But because of their 'I' ness remaining intact, despite the loss of a limb, as long as they are alive, their identity as a person remains unchanged, even though physically they may appear different.

"Your true self, this 'I'," I said, "is as pure as rainwater and filled with divine qualities such as mercy, tolerance, forgiveness, non-violence, respecting others, determination, enthusiasm, patience, happiness, humility, and many more. However, just as rainwater can become muddy after touching soil, our pure consciousness can be sullied by the negative influences within this world. Thus, sometimes we tend to manifest negative emotions such as anger, envy, frustration, depression, and so on."

At this point, I encouraged the children to contribute as many negative emotions as they could think of. As the children participated, the list of negative emotions grew long with words such as lonely, tense, revengeful, fearful, jealous, suicidal, ridiculed, feeling neglected, insulted, and many more.

## The cause of the disease

As I tried to explain the practical significance of knowing the concept of I-ness, I asked my students, "Can someone tell me as to *why* a person becomes diseased?" The most common answers I received were "Germs, bacteria, and viruses."

"Bacteria and viruses attack even a healthy person," I spoke, "but in normal conditions, a person's immune system is strong enough to combat a potential disease carrier. However, a person is more susceptible to falling sick when weak."

I asked my students, "Can you tell me when a person is most likely to become weak?"

"When they become *old*," a boy replied.

"Even old people can be physically fit," I defended, "they can have a disease-free body."

Another said, "When we don't get proper nourishment."

I agreed, "*Yes*, that is a valid reason, though I am looking for a cause that can make even a properly nourished person sick."

"When a person becomes weak in mind," a girl replied.

She provided me with the *precise* answer I was looking for. I got everyone to clap for her. Once the room quieted, I asked, "Who here desires a sound body and mind?"

Without an exception, everyone raised their hands. Everyone seemed to be on their toes, expecting some miracle to be revealed. I shared my miracle formula:

*If you want a healthy mind and thus, in turn, a healthy body, get rid of your negative emotions because they suck out your energy and make you sick, both mentally and physically.*

With this, I moved on to the last and most important part of my discussion: How to deal with our negative emotions mindfully.

## Mindfully dealing with negative emotions

Using the word 'Anger', I rephrased the four statements written on the board, which now read as follows:

THIS IS MY ANGER

It means:

1. 'I' am different.
2. My anger is different.
3. 'I' have an identity separate from my anger.
4. 'I' have a choice, how I want to deal with this anger.

To help the students effectively manage their negative emotions, I introduced a three-step formula: S-E-C; Scan, Empathise, Choose.

### Step 1: S – Scan

Children were asked to take a few deep breaths, after which they had to scan any negative emotion that they might be experiencing at the moment. I began to explain in detail, "This is the awareness part of the mindfulness practice. We may often get tormented by our negative emotions without even noticing them. Taking a pause and scanning our negative emotions is like diagnosing a disease before we can plan adequate treatment."

To illustrate my point, I used the example of a burn. I spoke, "When any part of our body gets burned, we experience pain, and instinctively, our body pulls itself away from the heat source. But what would happen to a person so oblivious of their body that despite a finger or any part of the body getting burned, they are not even aware of it? Similar is our situation when our mind becomes clouded, and we fail to even recognise, at first, the negative emotions that are taking a toll on us. By going through the process of emotion-scan, we can arrive at a platform from which we can effectively plan an appropriate solution."

### Step 2: E – Empathise

I further spoke, "The next step is to Empathise with your emotions. Empathy is the ability to understand how someone else feels. After scanning your negative emotions, don't deny them or don't try to run away from them. Your true self, the

'I', and your emotions are two different things. Keeping this in mind, try managing your emotions.

"Sometimes, a mindful acceptance could be everything you might need to do to tackle your emotions at a particular moment. It is like holding a crying baby and letting them know you are there for them. Just giving this feeling means a lot to the child. Give attention to your emotions, accept them, and reassure them that you will address them.

"Going through the process of scanning and empathising will give you sufficient clarity on how best to respond to the emotion efficiently. This brings us to the third and final step of mindfully addressing negative emotions."

### Step 3: C – Choose

Continuing, I said, "The crucial and final step is to decide on the approach you want to take towards your current negative emotion." At this stage, each child received a printed sheet with Table 5.1, listing probable solutions to manage their negative emotions. I read out the solutions to them, encouraging them to scan, empathise and then choose the most fitting option for their troubling feelings.

I also encouraged the children to come up with other probable solutions in the third column of the table, ideas they thought would be appropriate to deal with a particular emotion.

Table 5.1

| Emotion | Choose how you want to deal with this emotion | You can write other probable solutions |
|---|---|---|
| Anger | You can regulate this anger by practising mindful breathing, by counting from 1 to 5 and thus activating a pause button, by avoiding conflicting situations. | |
| Revenge | The feeling of revenge is like holding a burning coal in your hand; let it go. Those who try to harm others, in reality, hurt themselves. | |
| Loneliness, Hurt, Neglect, Guilt | Spend time with friends, reveal your heart to parents or someone close to you, spend time with pets, get involved in physical games or try to help others. | |
| Fear | Identify the root cause of fear, talk with guardians, offer prayers, and do mindful breathing. | |
| Getting Cheated | The saying goes, “If you cheat me once, shame on you. If you cheat me twice, shame on me.” Learn from the mistakes, be careful in future dealings, and do not let it happen again. | |
| Stress | Use mindful breathing, go for a walk, avoid excessive socialisation and gadgets, play physical games, and spend time talking to siblings, parents, or anyone close. | |

| **Emotion** | **Choose how you want to deal with this emotion** | **You can write other probable solutions** |
|---|---|---|
| Jealousy | Learn to appreciate others because your jealousy or envy is indirect appreciation. You feel envious of those who are better than you. | |
| Selfishness | Help others, give charity, and be grateful for everything you receive in life. | |

As the session drew to a close, I imparted some final thoughts to the group, "One aspect of choosing also has the choice to not identify with your negative emotions. Nonidentification does not mean denying your emotions. However, once you become consciously aware that your emotions are separate from your true self, you'll find yourself on a more effective platform for managing them.

"You are the maker of your destiny by the conscious choices you make in life. If applied mindfully, this principle of 'I'-ness will help you throughout your life. Instead, you will be equipped to help many others effectively deal with their negative emotions. When you get less marks, you feel low for a few days. But good marks alone are not success. Competence alone is not success. Competence, along with good character, is a success. Happiness is a success. Developing divine qualities is a success. Knowing how to manage your negative emotions is a success.

"A towering skyscraper can appear breathtakingly impressive," I said, "when viewed from the ground. Yet, from high above, it appears no larger than a mere matchbox. Similarly, the size of any painful emotion we experience in life is subjective and dependent on our perspective. By embracing the concept of "I" ness, we elevate our awareness and become less burdened by negative emotions. In such an expanded consciousness, one sees not just the external body but this 'I', the soul, which essentially is of the same nature in everyone, not only in human beings but all living entities. Just becoming mindful of this fact will stop us from discrimination based on colour, caste, creed, or religion. For those who are magnanimous, the entire world constitutes a family."

With this, I wrapped up the session. I thanked the children for their patient hearing and enthusiastic participation. We would meet again to continue with further sessions.

I returned to the monastery with a feeling of accomplishment for being able to make the children understand the vital concept of 'I' ness, around which, indeed, the whole practice of mindfulness is centred, not only to this age group but to people of all ages and walks of life. For the grownups, the first two steps, scanning the underflow of emotion and subsequently empathising with it, should reasonably bring them to an effective state of mind from where they should be able to choose an appropriate solution with a bit of conscience.

# 6

# *The Mystery of Past Life*

## Amazing 'I'

Our true self, the 'I' (also called Soul), is inherently driven by the pursuit of pleasure. Our body, consisting of subtle and gross elements, serves as an interface through which the 'I' tries to interact with the world to attain gratification. This 'I' is described as being atomic in size. Individually present in each body, this minute 'I' is responsible for sustaining life for humans and all living entities.

This 'I' is so powerful that it can even enable a giant elephant to run at an impressive speed of forty kilometres per hour. However, when the source of consciousness, the 'I' departs from the body, even twenty strong men might find it arduous to lift the deceased elephant. That is why 'I' is looked upon as someone who has amazing power.

## The beginning

The formation of the gross body around 'I' commences from the moment of conception in the mother's womb. Even in that state, what keeps the embryo alive is consciousness, which is the characteristic of this 'I'.

The embryo, nourished by the umbilical cord, grows every day, meaning it keeps increasing in terms of its contents of earth, water, fire, air, and ether. After birth, the body continues to develop, progressing through childhood, youth and adulthood. During adulthood, the body creates similar bodies through procreation. All through, what changes is the body, but the source of consciousness within this body, the 'I', remains unaltered.

After a certain age, the body starts becoming infirm and eventually meets with death. These six phases—birth, growth, maintenance, reproduction, dwindling, and death—are universal to all living beings. Till the time there is consciousness in the body, the five gross elements remain as a cohesive unit. As soon as the 'I' leaves the body, technically known as death, the five gross elements in the body start to disintegrate.

When the body dies, depending on cultural customs, it may be either cremated, buried, or left to decompose. In all cases, the five elements that once comprised the body merge back into their respective parent elements. For instance, when the gross body no longer exists, the space occupied by it is released. The ether element of the body merges with the universal ether. Solid element merges with the earth. The gaseous component combines with atmospheric air. Heat in the body gets dissipated into universal heat while the liquid parts join with atmospheric water.

## What goes to the next body after death?

When a person dies, we commonly pass comments like 'he has left' or 'he has gone away'. But *who* has left, or *who* has gone away?

Essentially, the gross body is still lying there, but what has left is the 'I', the real self that was keeping the body alive. The true self, the 'I', continues to exist beyond the confines of the body. Death is for the body and not for the 'I', which is eternal in nature.

Depending on its Karma and desires, this 'I' is reborn in another appropriate body after the death of the present one. The subtle part of the body consisting of mind and intelligence accompanies the 'I' to the next body. In the new body, the mind shapes fresh sets of impressions apart from carrying reminiscences of impressions from its previous life/lives. Many of our likes, dislikes, phobias, skills, and talents can be traced to have their roots in some previous births.

Besides storing and recollecting new information, the mind also has the essential function of forgetting. We may find it difficult to recall what we had for dinner two days back. Remembering what we had for dinner three months back will be almost impossible. It will be even more challenging to recall the details of all the events during our childhood.

Forgetfulness is a crucial aspect of our mind that enables normal functioning in our current life. Try to remember the moments of extreme emotional turmoil in your life. It could be due to the death of some close relative, emotional pain due to a broken relationship, or pain caused by someone insulting you terribly. Can you imagine living with the same intensity of emotional pain throughout your life?

However, the good thing is that with time, the intensity of those painful emotions keeps fading. That said, the mind also tends to forget the good experiences that were once cherished. Nevertheless, the impressions of those incidences and interactions—even though seemingly forgotten—are stored within our subconscious mind.

## Can we remember our past life?

The enigma of life and reincarnation has always fascinated humans, and it is not without reason. In some instances in early childhood, when the conditionings of the present life are not so deeply ingrained, a few children have been found to recollect past life events. Numerous authentic reincarnation stories from across the globe have been documented in books by various authors with substantial evidence.

Why only a chosen few and not all can remember their past lives remains an unanswered question. Nevertheless, these rare and proven cases of reincarnation provide convincing proof of the timeless essence of the self.

## Hypnotic regression

Regression refers to the act of returning to a former state. Hypnotic regression involves guiding an individual to delve into the deep-seated memories of their past, whether from this life or previous ones. This process requires a hypnotic therapist to lead the individual into a unique, guided deep sleep to unearth what lies buried in their subconscious mind. Throughout a hypnotic regression session, the patient's eyes remain closed, much like during regular sleep. However, their ears and mouth respond accordingly to the therapist's instructions.

Hypnotism can act as a healing therapy and aid individuals in overcoming trauma by allowing them to express deeply buried emotions and fears. This is accomplished by taking the individual's mind back to the original event that caused the acute emotion and then administering appropriate therapy to overcome it.

## My encounter with a hypnotic therapist

It was almost a decade ago. I was asked to speak at a condolence meeting for the grandmother of one of my students. After reciting some prayers, I spoke briefly about the eternal nature of the soul, the 'I'-ness aspect of our existence. Following my speech, a middle-aged gentleman, P. Devendra, came to me and introduced himself as a hypnotic therapist and shared his insight on the subject. He substantiated my statements about the eternal nature of our existence.

During the conversation, he shared the working mechanisms of hypnotism as well as some interesting incidents of hypnotic regression experienced by his clients. Over time, we met several times to explore the topic further. For the benefit of readers, I will share two real-life instances of hypnotic regression. The first involves regression within a person's current lifetime, while the second concerns past-life regression.

## Case 1:

### Regression within this lifetime

Gurleen, aged 21, had been experiencing breathing discomfort now and then for the past three years. She saw multiple doctors, but no one could diagnose any physical ailment in her. Some suggested it could be asthma, but she had not benefitted despite taking the prescribed treatment.

Someone suggested trying hypnotic regression to determine if the uneasiness in her breathing has its roots in some psychological problem in the past. Through some recommendations, her parents came across Devendra, who explained the process and scheduled a therapy session.

On the day of therapy, she was put in hypnotic slumber. The only connection she had at this stage was with her subconscious mind and with the voice of the therapist. She was completely unaware of the outside world during this time. From her present age, Gurleen was guided to go back in time to when she was 20, 19, and 18. At each stage, a series of questions were posed to determine if the current problem in her breathing originated from that particular period of her life. When her mind was directed to age 18, she was prompted to recollect all the occurrences that transpired during that year.

"I am studying in college," she spoke in a low voice, "staying in the hostel with my friends." Following some general occurrences, she proceeded to recount a specific event. "I am in my room in the hostel. It is around midnight. All of a sudden, around 8–10 girls entered the room. They took hold of me and started dragging me toward the bathroom. I am pleading with them to release me."

Therapist: "What happened after that?"

"They put me in the bathtub and opened the water tap," Gurleen spoke with much uneasiness.

Therapist: "Are they still holding you?"

"*Yes*. Help! The water has risen to my neck, and now it's pulling me under. I'm thrashing about, struggling to breathe."

Therapist: "How long did it continue?"

After a short pause, she responded with uncertainty, "I'm *not* sure. It feels like much time has gone by."

Therapist: "Are you still alive?"

She thinks awhile and answers, "Yes, but I am suffocating terribly. I can die at any moment." Palpitation and fear were evident in her body, even in her state of deep slumber.

Therapist: "Think deeply and speak whether what you are speaking of is a real event or a dream?"

Again, after a while, she spoke, "It is a dream."

The therapist spoke conclusively, "It is just a *dream*, Gurleen, which has consumed you for the last three years. Acknowledge that it is merely a figment of your imagination. Come out of this and say, 'It is just a dream which doesn't have any connection with my real life.'"

Still under the effect of hypnosis, she spoke in a low voice, "It is a dream that does not have any connection with my real life." Gradually, she was taken out of the effect of hypnosis. She looked relaxed and felt relief in her breathing. The cause of her breathing problem was traced back to a traumatic nightmare she experienced when she was 18, and since then, whenever she remembered that dream, which she took to be real, she would feel uneasiness and shortness of breath.

The entire therapy session was recorded on video. Through this therapy, her subconscious mind was made to acknowledge the reality of the situation. In the following weeks, she practised affirming to herself, "It was just a bad dream, don't take it seriously."

Eventually, her occasional difficulty in breathing disappeared.

**Case 2:**

## Past life regression

Past life regression is a form of hypnotism that takes a person on a journey back in time to recall events from their previous life. Initially, the person is gently guided into a deep slumber to retrieve memories from their current life. Their subconscious mind is then directed backwards through memories of adulthood, youth, and childhood, with the potential to recall events that occurred as early as 3, 2, 1......and finally 0. Delving deeper into the subconscious mind means attempting to uncover memories from a previous life.

This phase is crucial and needs to be handled very carefully by the hypnotic therapist because there exists a gap between the last death and the current birth. The transition of going back in time—from our present birth to our last death—involves a part in the journey when, for some time, the 'I' is without a gross body, accompanied only by the subtle body of mind and intelligence. The beginning of the 'I', taking shelter in this body, is counted from the very first day of conception within the womb. It is the presence of the 'I' which facilitates the entire body with all its complexities to be eventually formed around it, inside the womb.

During one of our conversations, Devendra shared with me an interesting story about past life regression. He recounted the experience of a woman from Kolkata, aged 32, who was eager to uncover her past life. Through hypnotic regression, her mind was guided to go back in time to her previous life. As she delved into her memories, she recalled being born in a village near Chittagong, now part of Bangladesh. She was the only daughter of a wealthy landlord, but her parents did not approve of her involvement in the Indian freedom movement, which she actively supported at the age of 19.

She further recalled the times when she left her home to journey alongside other comrades fighting for freedom. This went on for many years until India finally achieved independence in 1947. By then, she had aged considerably; her parents were *no* more. After independence, she took it upon herself to establish an orphanage in her village. For the remainder of her days, she dedicated herself to caring for the children at the orphanage, earning her the endearing title of '*Buddhi maa*' or the old Grandmother, as the village affectionately called her.

Once the woman had awoken from her hypnotic state, she listened to her recorded narrative. This sparked her curiosity to investigate whether the story was indeed true. Accompanied by her parents, she journeyed to the village in Bangladesh where her past supposedly took place. To her surprise, she discovered that an orphanage still stands there to this day, having operated since the country's Independence. At the entrance, a photo of an older woman adorned with a garland caught her attention. Beneath the image was inscribed—*Buddhi maa*.

After gathering information from the villagers, it was confirmed that 'Buddhi maa' was indeed a freedom fighter, as she had narrated during her hypnotic slumber. This discovery captivated her so much that she desired to spend the rest of her life serving in that orphanage. Somehow, by the intense persuasion of her parents and with the intervention of Devendra, the hypnotic therapist, she was brought back to her home in Kolkata.

On Saturday, December 14, 2013, the renowned Bangla daily *Anand Bazar Patrika* featured this story in its publication.

Devendra believes that although past life is a reality, people should not seek to know about it out of mere curiosity. He warns that gaining knowledge about one's previous life may reveal unsettling information that can disrupt a person's present functioning. As a result of this incident, Devendra no longer practices past life regression unless it is necessary for some healing purposes.

## What is a dream?

Wakefulness (*Jagriti*), dream (*Swapna*), and deep sleep (*Susupti*) are the three stages of awareness of our mind.

In a physically awake state (*Jagriti*), our awareness is acute. What we think and do has a direct correlation in this state. On the other hand, *Susupti* or deep sleep indicates sleeping without dreams. During this time, the body and mind both go into hibernation mode. Living a regulated lifestyle increases the likelihood of slipping into a deep, restful slumber. Just a few hours of deep sleep is sufficient enough to rejuvenate us both physically and mentally.

*Swapna* (dreaming) is an intermediate phase between wakefulness and deep sleep. Usually, during sleep, the awareness of the mind oscillates between deep sleep and a dreaming state (Fig. 6.1). In *Swapna*, much like deep sleep, we lose awareness of our physical identity, home, family, bank balance, and everything else. We are not even conscious of the

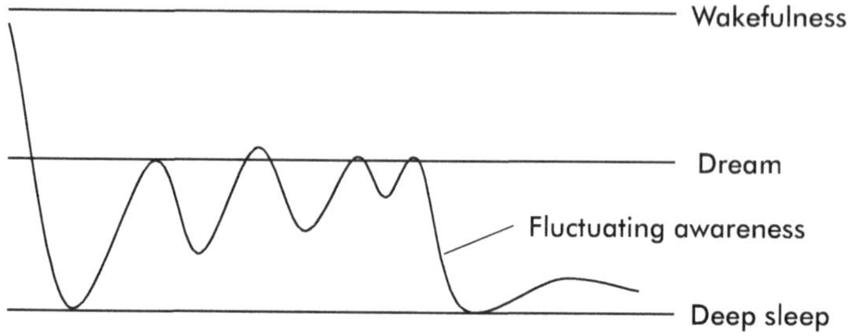


*Fig. 6.1*

fact that we are sleeping. However, in this state, though the physical body becomes dormant, the mind is active, painting vivid dreams based on our experiences while awake. For instance, if you have seen gold and a mountain, the mind may conjure up creativity and imagination to show you a golden mountain in the dream. The mind can also combine another experience, say seeing flying objects like aeroplanes or birds, to show you a flying golden mountain in the dream.

Sometimes, our subconscious mind can reveal past life impressions through our dreams, presenting us with unfamiliar experiences that we may not have encountered in this lifetime.

Apart from random dreams that may not significantly correlate with our current lives, there could also be dreams that surface to shape our buried emotions and unfulfilled desires. For example, if someone is extremely fearful of something, this emotion may surface in a dream in the form of a tiger chasing him. "Oh, there is a tiger! Save *me*!" he may cry out in sleep while another man, who is awake, may think, "Where is the tiger? Why is he crying out, Tiger?" But the one who is dreaming actually feels the real emotion when he screams, "The tiger has attacked me!"

There was a time when I needed to discuss a specific issue with one of my students, but he always managed to avoid me skillfully. One night, I had a dream in which I was severely reprimanding him. When I woke up, I chuckled at my dream, realising how my mind had extrapolated my emotions and manifested them as dream. Most likely, I would have never chastised him that harshly in reality.

Though a dream is not a reality, we don't think so while dreaming. At least for the time being, the dream becomes the only reality for us. The joys and sorrows experienced during a dream can manifest through visible signs, such as an increased heart rate, high blood pressure, shortness of breath, sweating, shouting, murmuring, smiling or laughing, etc.

In addition to the dream, as mentioned above, there are instances where a person may have a dream that predicts a future event. However, determining whether such uncommon occurrences should be termed as mere coincidence or 'something which holds a deeper meaning' is difficult to establish by the rules of conventional logic.

# 7

# *Our Conditioning*

## Forming a habit

Every interaction we have with the world around us leaves an imprint on the mind in the form of experiences. These experiences, in turn, give rise to specific thoughts and behavioural patterns.

Let's take the example of someone who decides to start with a morning walk on a regular basis. Say, on the very first day, they wake up early in the morning and successfully go for a walk. The invigorating experience of breathing in fresh and crisp morning air compounded with the serenity of the surroundings, the sweet melody of birds chirping, and breathtaking views of the rising sun leaves them spellbound. On top of all this is the sense of accomplishment that comes from being able to make a successful start in forming a good habit. The whole set of events eventually leads to a 'conditioning of the mind', which fosters a spontaneous proclivity to continue with this act of 'going for a morning walk' regularly.

Conversely, there may be someone else who also takes a resolution to start with a morning walk but, despite a few tries, struggles to rise early. Or even upon waking early, a sense of lethargy or reluctance may inhibit them from starting right away. Over time, repeated failures to kick off a successful routine may condition their mind to believe that, for the time being, "going for a morning walk isn't feasible for me."

We can swap the example of 'taking a morning walk' with any other instance of cultivating positive habits such as practising yoga, regulating our eating, being timely, avoiding procrastination, keeping our promises, following ethical principles, etc. In all such cases, whether or not an individual will succeed in adhering to their resolution to establish a new habit pattern will depend on the proclivity that their mind eventually develops towards those activities.

Similarly, how strongly susceptible one will be to adopting harmful habits will depend on how much their mind becomes attracted to, indifferent towards, or averse to those habits.

## What shapes our proclivity?

How does a proclivity towards anything originate in the mind?

If you trace back, you will find **freewill** to be the underlying root cause. Freewill is the individual's willingness to make personal choices independent of any external influence. At any given moment, we have the freedom to choose how we want to react—positively or negatively—which in turn gives rise to a particular proclivity inside us towards objects, people, or actions. As time passes, these preferences become ingrained in us, giving rise to a 'conditioning of our mind' that repeatedly prompts us to make the same choices. Consequently, it may appear as though our freedom to exercise freewill is camouflaged by this 'conditioning of our mind'.

To get a deeper insight, let us consider the example of an office party with an opportunity to consume alcohol. A person may use his freewill to say '*no*' to alcohol whenever he is obliged to attend such an event. This continual refusal or turning away from drinks would lead to a 'conditioning of the mind' of the person, which makes him indifferent to alcohol whenever it is available.

On the other hand, there could be a person who uses his freewill to consume alcohol at the very first opportunity, which in turn may lead to an increased proclivity in him to have a drink on subsequent occasions. Over time, this increased predisposition towards alcohol can lead to a particular 'conditioning of the mind', compelling the person to make the same choice consistently.

## To what extent are we free to choose?

How free is one in their choice to exercise freewill? This can be better understood through the analogy of a roller coaster ride.

Purchasing the ticket for the ride represents our freewill, for we are free to choose whether or not we want to take the ride. The roller coaster in motion represents a particular 'conditioning of our mind'. As soon as the ride starts, we are deprived of any freedom to come out of it, at least until the scheduled ride ends. Similarly, using freewill, we give shape to a particular conditioning of the mind that, over time, becomes so deep that it appears to take away our very choice to exercise the freewill.

## Conditioning in three modes

Conditioning of our mind is broadly divided into three categories: Conditioning under the influence of the Mode of goodness, the Mode of passion, and the Mode of ignorance.

Rising early, doing yoga, adhering to a healthy diet, carrying out our duties responsibly, appreciating others, feeling grateful, speaking words of wisdom, empathising with other's joys and sorrows, etc. are some examples of activities/ personality traits that represent a mind conditioned to be guided by the principles of goodness.

The objective of life for someone driven by the mode of passion is to always indulge in the pleasure of the senses to the fullest extent possible. Actions performed under this mode bring some ephemeral happiness that soon converts to distress. One such example is eating luxurious foods on a regular basis. Initially, such food feels delicious to the tongue, but eventually, it brings negative consequences—leading the person to become overweight or suffer from other health-related issues.

Some of the characteristics that mark ignorance are inertia, laziness, negligence, sleeping too much, procrastination and inability to see the truth. Actions such as taking intoxicants, gambling, breaking fidelity in marital relationships, etc., are examples of activities done under the influence of the mode of ignorance. Such acts are a source of misery from the beginning to the end, but out of illusion, the person mistakes the misery for happiness.

Traditionally, the modes are called *Satva guna* — mode of goodness, *Rajo guna* — mode of passion, and *Tamo guna* — mode of ignorance. The word *guna* means a string. Just as a puppeteer controls the puppet's movements through the strings attached, the three modes are like invisible strings attached to a person that govern their actions.

Some more characteristics and behaviours pertaining to a particular mode are listed below:

| **Mode** | **Some characteristics of the person attributed to the mode** |
|---|---|
| Mode of goodness (*Satva guna*) | Simple living, serene, truthful, kind, mindful, determined, helpful, honest, responsible, invests in building good relationships, sacrifices personal happiness for the good of others. |
| Mode of passion (*Rajo guna*) | Very competitive, over-ambitious, stressed, feels threatened by other's success, selfish, holds personal pleasure as the topmost priority. |
| Mode of ignorance (*Tamo guna*) | Sleeping too much, lazy, tendency to postpone, hopeless, morose. |

## ACTIVITY TIME

Classify the following personality traits under the correct category:

| | Select an option 1, 2 or 3 (1= Mode of goodness, 2= Mode of passion, 3= Mode of ignorance) |
|---|---|
| Insecure | |
| Aggressive | |
| Confused and directionless | |
| A stable state of mind | |
| Always frustrated | |
| Anxiety and lamentation | |
| Low tension, high energy | |
| Fearful and panicking | |
| Confident and happy | |
| Wise | |
| Propensity to cheat others | |
| Enthusiasm | |
| Patience | |

### The mix of modes

Throughout the day, these modes keep manifesting within us to varying degrees and proportions. Upon waking up, we may engage in activities such as going for a morning walk, exercising, meditation, taking a shower, etc. These activities are considered to be a part of the mode of goodness. However, as the day progresses, our actions are more influenced by the mode of passion. We may find ourselves rushing to work or the office worrying about unfinished assignments or deadlines, or feeling pressured to meet certain job targets. We also might have to deal with tasks of paying bills and similar duties. When we return home in the evening, the mode of ignorance tends to take over in the form of laziness, lethargy, and a strong desire for sleep.

In more practical terms, it may happen that during the morning hours, we are under the influence of 60% of mode of goodness along with 20% of mode of passion and 20% of mode of ignorance. It means that the prominent mode guiding our activity in this situation is the mode of goodness, while modes of passion and ignorance also being present, though to a lesser degree. For the same person at some other time in the day, the combination could be 20% mode of goodness, 20% mode of passion, and 60% mode of ignorance. In this situation, the mode of ignorance has taken superiority over the modes of goodness and passion.

Thus, it is common to see the mode of goodness, passion, and ignorance taking turns in prominence in our daily lives. At times, goodness takes the lead, overpowering passion and ignorance. Other times, passion dominates over goodness and ignorance, while ignorance can also overpower goodness and passion.

Nevertheless, while there still remains a struggle to keep an optimum balance between the modes, our lifestyle should be moulded in a way that is predominantly in the mode of goodness, as much as possible, as it offers us the benefits of good health, long-lasting happiness, inner satisfaction, peace of mind and overall wellbeing.

## Triggering of modes

Once, when I boarded the sleeper coach of an express train, I found my compartment in disarray. It appeared that the previous occupants had carelessly left their leftovers strewn across the floor. Seeing no recourse, I folded my legs and sat cross-legged on my seat. The other passengers also didn't mind much about the unclean state, probably because, for everyone, the journey was to end in a few hours or perhaps because there was no other choice.

However, much to our relief, soon after, we found a young boy arriving with a broom in hand, cleaning the entire coach. After this, the boy went to each compartment, soliciting money contributions for his cleaning services. However, when the boy came to our compartment, no one seemed to notice him at first. As he waited for a while, hoping for someone to contribute, a middle-aged gentleman offered him a few coins. And within no time, three more passengers, including myself, were compelled to provide a small contribution. A positive association infused the mode of goodness to awaken, at least for the time being, which helped some of us overcome the inertia that was stopping us from contributing initially.

## Modes shaping our inner nature

The modes are like the three primary colours: yellow, red, and blue. Symbolically, yellow represents mode of goodness, red represents mode of passion, and blue represents the mode of ignorance within us.

Just as we can make innumerable new colours by mixing the three primary colours in different proportions, the three modes mixed in various shades give rise to a particular type of conditioning in a person. These conditionings over a long period give rise to our inner nature reflected in our psycho-physical attributes, which are unique to every individual. For example, our preferences for food, clothing, music, hobbies, friends, literature, and vacation destinations are all exclusive to each of us.

Sometimes, despite having similar upbringings and supporting culture, two persons can have completely different inner natures. During my Value-based classes for children, I encountered identical twin brothers who looked so similar that I had to give them name batches in every class to ensure I identified them correctly. But when it came to their likings or talents, in terms of sports, academics, or culinary preferences, there were striking differences between them.

Our upbringing in this life plays a significant role in ascertaining our inner nature, but some of these attributes could also be carry-overs from our previous lives. Even though identical twins have similar physical bodies, their subtle bodies comprising mind and intelligence could be considerably different because it is the result of their subtle bodies journeying through different exposures and experiences in their previous lives.

Traditionally, understanding a child's inner nature at an early age plays a vital role in deciding what personality type would best emerge from them. For instance, some could excel in music while others can do well in arts; some could have good interpersonal skills, while others may lack them. Some could be good at logic, some could excel in sports, while others could have the inclination and inquisitiveness to search for a deeper meaning in life. Some could also have a mixture of two or more of these talents present in them in various degrees.

In essence, having a good understanding of one's existing inner nature will make one aware of their strengths as well as limitations. The next mindful approach would be to work in harmony with one's strengths and overcome limitations.

## Determine your profile

Take some time to determine your profile based on the influence of the three modes in your life. Complete the survey below.

Circle the number that best represents your response.

0— Strongly disagree
1— Disagree
2— Neutral
3— Agree
4— Strongly agree

1 I am satisfied with my life.

0 1 2 3 4

2 I often feel like a victim.

0 1 2 3 4

3 My job is a source of anxiety.

0 1 2 3 4

4 I am a vegetarian because I respect life, even animals and birds.

0 1 2 3 4

5 I like to gamble.

0 1 2 3 4

6 I often feel fearful of people around me.

0 1 2 3 4

7 Regardless of what I acquire or achieve, I have an uncontrollable desire to obtain more.

0 1 2 3 4

8 Money is everything to me.

0 1 2 3 4

9 I envy the success of other people.

0 1 2 3 4

10 I often neglect my health to achieve my goals.

0 1 2 3 4

11 I sleep long hours.

0 1 2 3 4

12 Cleanliness is very important to me.

0 1 2 3 4

13 I find myself struggling with time management.

0 1 2 3 4

14 I often put off or delay my responsibilities.

0 1 2 3 4

15 I eat and sleep at regulated times.

0 1 2 3 4

16 When I speak, I try not to irritate others.

0 1 2 3 4

17 I like to boast about my achievements.

0 1 2 3 4

18 I often feel emotionally unbalanced.

0 1 2 3 4

19 I am constantly dissatisfied with my position in life.

0 1 2 3 4

20 I sometimes cheat people.

0 1 2 3 4

21 I cannot maintain fidelity in my marital relationship.

0 1 2 3 4

22 Being truthful is extremely important to me.

0 1 2 3 4

23 I give regular charity.

0 1 2 3 4

24 I often sacrifice my pleasure to please others.

0 1 2 3 4

25 I often neglect my responsibilities to my family.

0 1 2 3 4

26 I give quality time to my family.

0 1 2 3 4

27 In my life, I usually experience deep happiness that is not dependent on anything external.

0 1 2 3 4

28 I get angry quite often.

0 1 2 3 4

29 I am currently struggling with an addiction, physical or psychological.

0 1 2 3 4

30 I can do anything to get what I like.

0 1 2 3 4

The process of assessment is provided on the page after the next. Please be honest not to jump to the evaluation before you complete the test above. This act in itself will fall under the mode of goodness.

## How to assess your test on the three modes of nature:

Fill the table below with your answers (The number you circled in the test sheet). Write your reply against the question number indicated in Tables A, B, & C.

| Table A | |
|---|---|
| Question no | Your answer to this question (the number you circled in the test sheet) |
| 1 | |
| 4 | |
| 12 | |
| 15 | |
| 16 | |
| 22 | |
| 23 | |
| 24 | |
| 26 | |
| 27 | |
| | Sum Total of above answers:<br><br>G =............. |

| Table B | |
|---|---|
| Question no | Your answer to this question (the number you circled in the test sheet) |
| 3 | |
| 7 | |
| 8 | |
| 9 | |

| Table B | |
|---|---|
| Question no | Your answer to this question (the number you circled in the test sheet) |
| 10 | |
| 13 | |
| 17 | |
| 20 | |
| 28 | |
| 30 | |
| | Sum Total of above answers:<br><br>P =............ |

| Table C | |
|---|---|
| Question no | Your answer to this question (the number you circled in the test sheet) |
| 2 | |
| 5 | |
| 6 | |
| 11 | |
| 14 | |
| 18 | |
| 19 | |
| 21 | |
| 25 | |
| 29 | |
| | Sum Total of above answers:<br><br>I =............ |

Table A contains questions that belong to the mode of goodness category. Table B includes questions that fall under the mode of passion. Lastly, Table C comprises questions that pertain to the mode of ignorance category.

Your mode of goodness score (in %) = (G/T) × 100
Your mode of passion score (in %) = (P/T) × 100
Your mode of ignorance score (in %) = (I/T) × 100

*Where* T = G + P + I

Of course, ascertaining the influence of modes in our lives needs a much more detailed analysis and is much more personalised and time-consuming than the method adopted above. However, for now, going through the above survey will give the readers a sufficient idea about the predominant mode influencing their lives. The next mindful progression that one should make should be to do anything necessary to elevate oneself from the mixed mode of ignorance and passion, striving to attain a state that closely approximates the mode of goodness.

# 8

# *Modes in Everyday Life*

This chapter will delve into the important elements of mindfulness practices that can enhance our health, happiness, and inner satisfaction by elevating our consciousness and, thus, lifestyle to the mode of goodness.

Some of the principles discussed in this chapter have their origins in Ayurveda, a term that translates to "knowledge (*Veda*) of life (*ayu*)."

## 1. Mindful eating

Maintaining good health is one of the most valuable assets we can possess, and one of the key ways to achieve this is by adhering to a comprehensive eating plan. Food serves three main purposes: satisfy the mind, nourish the body, and eradicate hunger.

Depending on how it affects the body and mind, the food we consume can be divided into three categories: foods in the mode of goodness, foods in the mode of passion, and foods in the mode of ignorance. The foods under the mode of goodness increase the duration of life and give strength, health, happiness, and satisfaction. Some examples of unprocessed food under this category are fruits, nuts, vegetables, cereals, pulses, milk, and milk-based products.

Foods under the mode of passion have a sharp taste, i.e., they are either too sour, salty, hot (chilli), pungent, or produce burning sensations. Such foods can cause harm by reducing the mucus in the stomach, leading to diseases. This category *also* includes fast foods, packaged preserved foods, and foods high in fat and spices.

Food that is decomposed, putrid, or contains flesh, meat, and eggs is categorised as being in the mode of ignorance. All types of intoxicants also fall under this category.

## Stages leading to mindful eating

### I. Mindfulness in selecting the ingredients

Our food consumption typically involves three stages: procuring the ingredients, preparing or cooking them, and finally, consuming the meal. Choosing and consuming ingredients that fall under the mode of goodness can lead to a happier and healthier life than those who opt for foods that fall under the mode of passion or ignorance.

The following table contains a broad guideline:

| Foods in the mode of ... | Some examples | Advised consumption |
|---|---|---|
| Goodness | Foods based on cereals, pulses, beans, vegetables, fruits, milk, and its derivatives. | The majority of our dietary consumption should fall within this particular category. |
| Passion | Foods rich in fat, very spicy foods, fast foods, etc. | Eat moderately |
| Ignorance | All varieties of meat, fish, and eggs, all intoxicating and addictive things like cigarettes, hard drinks, etc. | Avoid completely |

## II. Mindfulness while cooking

The food we consume, potentially, is the greatest healer not only for our body but also for our mind. When we eat, what goes inside the body is not only the food's gross content but also the cook's subtle consciousness, which subtly imbues the food while cooking. Food prepared with love and attention is better for the body than food cooked carelessly.

Home food, or one's mother's cooking, is most commonly held as comfort food—something that gives inner satisfaction and happiness. It has been scientifically proven that certain foods can make a person feel instantly better and happier.

Cooking is a divine act, especially when it is for others. It should be carried out with the thought of pleasing others. If the cook has a disturbed mind or is angry or unhappy while cooking, the negativity seeps into the food cooked, and similar emotions will be transferred to all those who eat the food. Even if you cook it for yourself, do it in a relaxed and happy mood. A clean and well-arranged kitchen helps keep a positive mind while cooking.

Consuming cooked food as fresh as possible is important since its vitality and energy content diminish over time. Refrigeration of cooked food and its subsequent reheating should be avoided, for it can cause substantial loss of nutrients. These foods fail to provide adequate nourishment for the body and do not offer a sense of satisfaction for the mind.

As per Ayurveda, it is recommended that ingredients be exposed to atmospheric oxygen during the cooking process. That way, the nutrients in the food are preserved to the maximum extent. When food is pressure-cooked, it results in a loss of nutrients. Hence, the use of a pressure cooker should be kept to a minimum.

It is advisable to refrain from using microwave ovens for cooking or reheating food due to their potentially harmful effects.

Cooking with clay utensils is highly recommended as they aid in preserving nutrients to the maximum extent. The following best options are brass, iron, or steel utensils. Cooking in aluminium (or its alloy) vessels should be avoided as some may have the potential to make the food toxic.

Non-stick pans with Teflon coating can pose health risks when the coating breaks down and mixes with food over time. It is best to avoid using them.

## III. Mindfulness while eating

### 45 minutes of happiness

Once, I was invited to a student's home to share some ideas for good living. It was an evening gathering of family and friends. There were around twenty of them—comprising children, women, men, and older adults. After doing the initial chants and prayers, I chose to speak on 'Mindfulness for happier living.' Eventually, I inquired, "Could you share with me the amount of time you genuinely feel happy on a daily basis?"

As others pondered the answer, an elderly gentleman confidently responded with "*45 minutes*" without hesitation.

Everyone and I were pleasantly surprised to hear the old gentleman's precise answer. Without waiting for my response, he explained that he experiences 15 minutes of pure happiness during each meal—breakfast, lunch, or dinner.

The room erupted with laughter after hearing such a sincere response. Throughout the years, I've come to appreciate the value of preserving the *wise words* of older individuals. It's been over a decade since the incident, but that interaction remains vivid in my recollection. Seeing people's lifestyles today, I wonder how many are fortunate enough to experience just 45 minutes of pure happiness each day, generated by mindful eating.

## When to eat

It's advisable to consume food when you're feeling really hungry, as anything eaten at this point gets digested with ease. By regulating your body clock, you can train it to stimulate your appetite at specific times of the day.

The human digestive system is synchronised to work according to the sun's movement. Our digestive power is strongest around noon. As the sun sets, our digestion begins to weaken, making it wise to have dinner earlier in the evening.

## Prepare a proper mindset

The type of consciousness we have while eating plays a vital role in getting our food digested. Maintaining a dedicated meal time to eat at home or in the office is important. Avoid multitasking, such as watching TV, chatting on the phone, working on a laptop, or giving instructions. There could be an interesting conversation if others are eating along with you. However, it's important to steer clear of contentious or negative subjects to savour the moment of mindful eating fully.

It's recommended to eat while sitting down. Eating while standing or lying down can impede proper digestion. It's beneficial to take a few mindful breaths (informally) before beginning to eat. This helps in calming the mind and bringing awareness to the act of eating.

Watch all the items on your plate before diving in. Our fast-paced modern lifestyle often prompts us to consume food quickly. However, it's important to take time with your meals. If you tend to eat hastily, make a conscious effort to slow down. This facilitates sufficient time to break down the food properly before gulping it and enhances the enjoyment of each flavour, both of which are important for the body to secrete appropriate enzymes required for effective digestion.

### How much to eat

When practising mindful eating, it's important to recognise when you've had enough food. Take the time to mindfully assess whether or not your hunger has been satisfied. If you answered yes, it's recommended to start wrapping up the meal. Admittedly, putting into action the idea of stopping oneself from eating, despite the food being delectable, is easier said than done. But with conscious practice over time, it is possible to become more efficient at it. Eating slowly and mindfully helps in this regard.

Ayurveda suggests that a complete meal should occupy only half of the stomach. One-fourth of the space should be reserved for drinking water, and the remaining one-fourth should be kept vacant to facilitate the proper mixing of the food. This helps maintain an active fire of digestion in the stomach.

One should be mindful of food waste and should take steps to stop it. One way to do this is by being conscious of the amount of food we put on our plates.

### Feel grateful

Feel grateful for having gotten this opportunity to eat. Express gratitude to all those who played a role in bringing the food to your plate. This includes the hardworking farmers, the helpful insects and organisms that aided in the growth of crops, vegetables, or fruits, the individuals who sourced and procured the ingredients, the person who prepared the meal, and the one who served it to you. Showing appreciation to everyone involved is a thoughtful gesture. It's worth noting that many bacteria in the stomach play a significant role in breaking down the food we consume, so if you desire, you can express gratitude to them also.

Be mindful that food is a precious gift. Take the time to express your gratitude and appreciation to Mother Nature. Show thanks to the Supreme Being who provides nourishment for all living creatures.

One may utter a humble prayer, wishing every being on this planet to be well-fed and nourished: *May there be no hostility or animosity amongst individuals, and may peace prevail in all corners of the world.*

## IV. Drinking water mindfully

Water makes up almost 60% of the human body. Therefore, it is crucial to drink adequate water daily to avoid dehydration and effectively eliminate toxins from the body. Being mindful of both the amount and method of water consumption is essential.

Ideally, the minimum amount of water a person should drink varies with weight. Ayurveda recommends the following amount for individuals weighing 50 kg or more in tropical climates:

> The minimum daily water intake in litres = (Body weight in kilograms divided by 10) minus 2.5.
>
> Thus, a person weighing 60 kg should ideally drink at least 3.5 litres of water daily, while those weighing 80 kg should strive for a minimum of 5.5 litres.

When engaging in regular physical activity, the body naturally signals a need for appropriate water consumption. However, in case you don't have a habit of drinking enough water, it would be wise to gradually work towards improving this aspect of your routine. Remember to make a conscious effort to see progress over time.

It is crucial for those who work in air-conditioned environments to actively monitor their water consumption level, as their natural thirst signals may occur less frequently. Most people need help to tell how much water they drink every day. So, keeping a standard measuring bottle to know how much water is consumed daily is recommended. This is the awareness part of a mindful act.

Drinking as much water as possible after waking up is recommended. Drinking water 45 minutes before a meal gives rise to a strong appetite. However, during mealtime, it is best to avoid or limit water intake as it slows down the fire of digestion in the stomach. Post-eating, water may be consumed after 45 minutes.

Water purified by reverse osmosis (RO) should be avoided since, apart from removing impurities, it also removes some essential minerals from the water, tending to make it acidic. Ideally, the pH value of drinking water should be close to 7, with a slight preference towards a value slightly above 7.

## Correct pose for drinking water

It is advisable to drink water while sitting down. Consuming water with your head held high (Fig. 8.1) may exert unnecessary strain on the thyroid glands, which could potentially result in thyroid-related health issues. Therefore, it is best to avoid this posture when drinking water.

Drinking from a glass or a cup, as shown in Fig. 8.2, is recommended as it allows the neck to remain relaxed while drinking.

*Fig. 8.1*

*Fig. 8.2*

Incorporating all the principles of mindful eating discussed here, although initially may seem time-consuming, with consistent effort and practice, becomes a natural part of our daily routine.

## 2. Mindful sleeping

The human body has a natural emotional and physical healing mechanism called sleep. Good sleep is the ultimate remedy for the body's well-being. When feeling tired, sleeping anywhere is possible, regardless of the conditions. Engaging in good physical activities during the day, like yoga, walking, cycling, playing outdoors, swimming, etc., can aid in achieving restful sleep.

It's important to be aware of our sleep habits, including the amount and timing of our sleep. Too much sleep can lead to lethargy, while too little can result in restlessness. Getting 6–7 hours of sleep per night is generally recommended for good health, although sleep needs may vary depending on age group and health conditions. Consistently staying up late at night can lead to chronic health issues. It's advisable to go to bed early and wake up early, ideally before sunrise.

It's crucial to sleep in a well-ventilated place since our brain replenishes its oxygen supply during sleep. In contrast to central air conditioning systems commonly found in industrial spaces, which use a regulated duct to mix fresh air with the circulating air, split or window ACs installed in homes do not have a designated system for bringing in fresh air. The only sources of fresh air are the occasional opening of doors or windows and small gaps in the room. The air you exhale, cough, or sneeze remains circulating in the room. As a result, even with sufficient sleep, your body may not fully relax in such a room. Thus, ensuring that the room is adequately ventilated before sleeping is vital while using such air conditioning.

It is advisable to distance oneself from electronic devices like mobile phones when sleeping. The radiation disrupts the natural slowing of body processes, which can hinder achieving deep sleep. A helpful tip for falling asleep quickly is to take a few mindful breaths while reclining.

Ayurveda recommends sleeping with your head towards the east and feet towards the west for optimal sleep. It is advised to avoid sleeping with your head facing north.

### 3. Mindfulness in speech

The way we speak is a reflection of our character. Therefore, being conscious of our words and how we articulate them is vital.

Avoid using words that intentionally agitate others. When we use such words, we also end up feeling agitated ourselves. Humour, jokes, and fun are all important parts of life, but they should never be used in a way that disrespects or harms others. Of course, we have a right to discuss the faults of others, but only constructively and beneficially. Being mindful of our speech helps us refrain from saying rude or hurtful things, even in moments of frustration.

Being truthful is an important pillar of mindful speech. No one suffers more than someone who knows he is not being true. Truthfulness means to be free from duplicity, i.e. what we think, say, mean and do are all aligned.

We need to be mindful not to become a carrier of negativity by constantly talking about the faults of others. It sucks out our positive energy. This world is full of flaws, but we have the choice to develop a mindful perception. Being mindful helps us recognise that constantly finding faults and being overly critical of those around us should not become our default behaviour. How we speak is closely tied to our level of consciousness, as it can elevate or lower it. Mindful speech leads us towards the mode of goodness, while an unmindful one moves us towards the mode of passion or ignorance.

Be a honey bee and not a fly. It's fascinating how a fly can be drawn to the tiniest bit of trash in a garden bursting with beautiful flowers. However, even amidst a pile of garbage, a single sweet-smelling flower will still capture the attention of a honey bee, causing it to become completely oblivious to its surroundings.

## 4. Mindfulness in dealing with others

I had the pleasure of meeting Bonnie nearly six years ago when Rajesh, an acquaintance, introduced us during his visit to my monastery. Bonnie and Rajesh were childhood friends who grew up in the picturesque town of Kalimpong, nestled in the foothills of the Himalayas in northern West Bengal, India.

Despite being in his early 40s, Bonnie appeared younger than his actual age. He enjoyed conversing and expressing his ideas on the virtues of a wholesome life. Meeting him would influence anyone with strong views and convictions on positive life values. Born of a Hindu mother and a Christian father and raised in Kalimpong, the home of many Buddhist monasteries, Bonnie had developed a good understanding of the principles of Hinduism, Christianity, and Buddhism.

We regaled each other with our experiences of wholesome living. Meandering through multiple aspects of life, our conversation veered to the importance of developing meaningful relationships.

"In my experience, I have discovered that a deep and fulfilling relationship is the biggest emotional need of every individual. The advent of the internet and virtual social media associated with it has distanced people more than ever before," said Bonnie.

"I agree," I replied, "our desire to stay connected with the world often causes us to neglect those physically present in our lives. It may be effortless to acquire fifty online social media friends in a day, but maintaining a single friendship for fifty years can be challenging."

"Yes," Bonnie added, "establishing a long-lasting relationship demands years of investment in building a strong foundation. However, like any other commitment, it must weather the harsh test of time to endure. Such relationships must confront and overcome intolerance, misunderstandings, conflicts, and prejudice."

He paused before saying, "I have a personal objective to make at least five trustworthy friends with whom I can share anything—friends I can rely on without a second thought and without being judged, even if I need to cry in their presence."

Bonnie let out a sigh and sadly stated that a vast majority of individuals in this world do not have any friend who falls under this particular category.

Curious, I asked, "How many friends do *you* have in this particular category?"

He raised the fingers of his right hand in a gesture of accomplishment, indicating *three*. He then placed his arm on Rajesh's shoulder and spoke, "One of them is Rajesh, who is much more than just a friend to me."

Rajesh, who had been mostly silent until now, suddenly beamed with a smile that almost reached his ears. It was a privilege to witness the genuine warmth in their relationship.

Sometime later in the same year, Bonnie shifted to Tokyo, where he opened a restaurant serving Indian cuisine. This was his dream project: to start a restaurant where guests would feel welcomed and at home rather than just being customers who enjoyed the food. He named it '*Downtown B's Indian Kitchen*'. His visitors were a mixed crowd of Japanese and tourists from India and other countries.

Keeping in mind the ethnicity and interest of visitors, he would play suitable soothing music in the restaurant to enhance their dining experience. He would sometimes inquire about their music preferences and play tunes aligned with their choices. Bonnie had trained his team members to treat every visitor as a personal guest. Regarding the food, he meticulously attended to every detail to ensure the utmost satisfaction of all guests. He would share with me, on the phone, anecdotes about his visitors. Here is one such story:

One day, Bonnie noticed that an elderly Indian couple had been sitting in his restaurant for quite a while. The expression on their faces suggested concern. Bonnie had one of his team members speak to this couple, who found out that the couple were waiting for their daughter to come and pick them up. She would reach around 5 p.m.

Since it was only early afternoon, Bonnie conversed with the couple and kindly offered to provide transportation to their desired destination, whether it be their hotel or elsewhere.

The old couple explained that their daughter worked in the United States and was coming to Tokyo in the evening for a two-week assignment. They had come from India to be with her for the next two weeks. Their son from Australia was also joining them later in the night. Since they had nowhere else to go, their daughter suggested that the couple go directly to the restaurant from the airport and wait for her there.

Bonnie made every effort to ensure the couple felt at ease and never felt like an inconvenience. He got some special soup made for them and regularly checked on them.

As anticipated, at around 5 p.m., the couple's daughter arrived at the restaurant directly from the airport. She took the luggage from her parents and started stowing it in the vehicle. Bonnie was curious to know if their daughter had visited the restaurant earlier.

"What made you select *this* restaurant for your parents?" Bonnie asked her, "Have you dined here before?"

"This is my first time in Tokyo," she replied, "I was browsing the internet for an Indian restaurant where my parents could dine and wait for me till I arrived. The reviews of your restaurant on the internet gave me the feeling that this would be the right place for them. Customers in all other restaurants talked about the quality and taste of the food, but in the reviews of your restaurant, more than the food, your customers complimented the homely feeling they received here. This was *precisely* the kind of place I had been looking for."

The elderly couple felt immensely grateful for the kindness and attention they had received in a place far from their own home. Thanking Bonnie profusely, the family of three left the restaurant.

Earning is undoubtedly a crucial aspect of running a business, but these extra personal touches are something Bonnie does out of love rather than obligation. The rules of reception state that a person with nothing to offer his guest should be good enough to provide at least a place to sit, a glass of water for drinking, and some sweet words. Bonnie did all of that and more. He says, "Even a small gesture to genuinely please someone without being asked to can mean a lot to others. And this, in turn, brings its reward, with a happiness and inner satisfaction that can't be put into words."

Later, while going through the pages of ancient wisdom, I discovered the six principles of loving exchanges between two individuals. These are: giving and receiving gifts, revealing one's mind in confidence and inquiring confidentially, and receiving and offering food. I was delighted by the striking similarities between these six principles and those followed by

Bonnie in his day-to-day life—to bring joy to his guests and everyone he encounters.

Each individual has a distinct psycho-physical nature that may not lend oneself to being as expressive as someone like Bonnie. But there should be a few or at least one in the inner circle of our life with whom we can experience a deep, fulfilling relationship. And achieving this requires selfless intention in our interactions with the person and the investment of quality time.

Once, I messaged Bonnie to ask if he ever had any serious misunderstanding with Rajesh.

He replied: To *me*, success in a relationship means making a conscious decision to work through our differences and persist even when it may seem easier to give up.

## ACTIVITY TIME

Take a moment to contemplate the individuals closest to you in your life (These are the individuals you can confide in and rely on to have your back in any circumstance. Typically, those individuals consist of close family members or long-time friends).

Write their name(s) and your relationship with each.

______________________________

______________________________

______________________________

What are some ways to apply the principles of the six loving exchanges to enhance the fulfilment of this relationship?

________________________________________________

________________________________________________

________________________________________________

________________________________________________

________________________________________________

________________________________________________

________________________________________________

________________________________________________

If you do not have someone who fits the category above, identify the individual who is the most likely candidate to fulfil those requirements. Afterwards, think of ways to strengthen and enhance this relationship.

________________________________________________

________________________________________________

________________________________________________

________________________________________________

________________________________________________

________________________________________________

________________________________________________

________________________________________________

# 9

# *Our Innate Need*

## The chariot of our body

There is an analogy of our gross body being compared to a chariot drawn by the five horses. The five horses represent our five knowledge-acquiring senses. The surface on which the horses are running is compared to the five sense objects. The reins are being compared to the mind that controls the horses. The charioteer who holds the reins represents our intelligence. The passenger is our real self, 'I' (the soul), the source of consciousness in the body. As a charioteer acts according to the command of the passenger, ideally, intelligence is supposed to be subordinate to the soul.

To ensure smooth manoeuvring of the chariot, the charioteer must have a firm grip on the reins to guide the horses effectively. On the same analogy, for a proper involvement of the body in terms of an appropriate sense engagement, a sound intellect must govern the mind, which in turn regulates the senses.

However, just as horses rebel if you try to control them forcefully, the senses will torment you even more if they are too deprived of enjoyment. Both extravagance and neglect are condemned when it comes to fulfilling the demands of the senses. Hence, the need is for regulation to satisfy the senses with proper engagement, mainly in terms of a healthy (as well as tasty) diet, good sleep, and meaningful recreation.

The needs of intelligence and mind are satisfied by following the guidelines set forth in the words of the wise. However, the soul's need gets satisfied only by experiencing selfless love, which we seek in everyone in this world. The purest form of such a fulfilling love found in this world is a mother's love towards an infant. She has to remain alert and awake practically round the clock, sacrificing her comforts to cater to the baby's needs. All she desires in return is for her little one to be happy and healthy.

## Identity crisis

Once, Amit, my batchmate, visited me at the monastery. It was a nostalgic experience as we hadn't seen each other in over a decade since graduating. We reminisced about our college days, sharing the good and challenging times we had shared during our four years in the college hostel. We were both eager to catch up on each other's lives since graduation. Amit went on to become a chief engineer in the merchant navy. As for me, after a brief career in sailing and further higher studies, I was attracted to lead the life of a monk.

After random conversations mostly centred on the lives of our other batchmates, Amit spoke of some social welfare work he had recently got involved with. He was working on a de-addiction campaign for the villagers in certain areas of Jharkhand and West Bengal. For me, it was a mixed feeling of happiness and a surprise because, since my college days, I had known him as a chain smoker. It piqued my curiosity to find out, of *all* things, what led him to start a de-addiction campaign.

Even before I could enquire, Amit shared, "I started smoking by chance. Want to know *how*?"

"I'm curious," I responded.

"*Honestly*, I didn't like it," Amit spoke with a feeling of resentment, "when I started smoking for the first time, during the beginning days of our hostel life. But I had an identity crisis then. When I started smoking, I found my batchmates identifying me as a macho man. And this led to a thought inside me—good or bad doesn't matter; at least I have a unique identity for myself now—and this led to my downfall. It took me many years to realise the harm I did to my body to maintain a meaningless identity. For over a year, I have completely given up all sorts of intoxication. Instead, whenever I am free, I help others to leave these destructive habits."

This led me to explain the concept of 'I'-ness to Amit, "Not only you, everyone in this world is searching for an identity. An identity that truly makes one happy and content. However, those who fail to connect with their inner self often turn to external sources for validation, often in a wrong way through improper habits."

Amit nodded in agreement as I continued with my thoughts, "You know, a musk deer spends his entire life searching for the source of the fragrance, not realising that the fragrance of the musk is coming from his own navel. Similarly, all external pleasures that a person looks for, either in intoxicants or, for that matter, in money, fame, position, or anything of this world, at best, can titillate our mind and senses for a limited time. However, a person lacks identity unless there is inner fulfilment."

I congratulated Amit for being amongst the fortunate few who could reverse this vicious cycle of intoxicating habits.

He told me he was also working with prisoners in a few jails, teaching them meditation and yoga. He extended an invitation for me to join him whenever possible.

"It would be my privilege to do that," I told him. I was feeling innate satisfaction for reconnecting with an old friend who shared similar values and principles as me. With that, we said our goodbyes, promising to be in frequent touch with each other.

After Amit left, I couldn't help but contemplate how many others like him might be ensnared by detrimental habits in the pursuit of a meaningless identity. In all such cases, the person needs to strengthen their intelligence by practising a lifestyle that gives them pleasure that is deep, satisfying, and enduring and helps them to connect to their inner self.

## What compels us to act wrongly?

It was a Sunday morning. I had just finished my workshop on "Mindful Parenting." It was a mixed audience of mothers, fathers, and a few grandparents. Guardians were still coming to me to discuss specific points related to the workshop or their wards. The conversations went on for quite some time. In the end, Aaryan's mother came up to me.

Aaryan was in grade 6 and was part of my weekly Value Education classes. His mother was seeking guidance regarding Aaryan's father, who had developed an intense addiction to a certain online game in the last few months. Most of the time, he would remain locked in his room, playing and chatting with his gaming friends over the internet. He would only occasionally come out of his room for meals or bare minimum necessities.

She confided, "My husband runs a business that he inherited from his father. Ever since becoming obsessed with this online game, he has gradually reduced going to the office. So much so that he has not stepped out of the house for the last two months; he left it to the employees to run the business, and the company is going through losses. As a consequence, our family finance is in a precarious condition. He has become completely oblivious to everything except this game, practically day in and day out."

So far, I heard many parents complain about their wards being addicted to the internet or mobile games. However, this was the first time I encountered a situation where an adult behaved so.

I asked whether she tried talking to her husband about the issue.

"Whenever I tried talking to him about this, it has led to serious confrontations," she said, "He does not like his privacy to be questioned or invaded."

"How is his relationship with Aaryan?" I asked, "Does he spend time with him?"

She expressed her concern, "It is limited to some basic interactions. Previously, my husband used to talk and play with Aaryan, but since this internet game addiction has taken over, he has completely stopped spending time with him. Even between us, communication is limited to only the basic necessities. He barely talks to me. The entire responsibility of chores, purchases, and handling finances, along with taking care of Aaryan and his studies, has come upon me. The situation at home is tense and hopeless. Both financial and relationship insecurity are gnawing at me, making it very difficult to continue in this house."

After a brief pause, she said, "I feel the need to separate from my husband and raise Aaryan on my own."

I could feel the *extreme* helplessness in her voice.

I asked if any close friends or family members could help her husband in this situation.

"Yes, there are few of them," she sighed, "but they are struggling with their own issues. On top of it, no one wants to get involved with someone's personal matters even if they are seemingly close to you."

I asked how she planned on managing if they separated. She admitted that she was unsure at the moment and might have to find a job. Her tone was hopeless and downcast. I had an intuition and found the courage to ask, "Do you get suicidal thoughts?"

She kept her head low and nodded in affirmation.

A pensive moment prevailed. I broke the silence, "Have you thought what would happen to Aaryan if you were no more?"

"Just this thought stops me from taking my life," her voice was almost a whisper.

I implored her to give up the idea of suicide and also suggested that she should not separate. I felt it would be too much of a financial and social burden on her to raise Aaryan as a single mother. I encouraged her to hold onto hope. I had faith that the situation would improve. *How*? It was not clear to me as of now. Perhaps perseverance was the key.

Sometimes, all you can do is provide someone with a glimmer of hope to go on. At times, mindful hearing is the only thing you can offer and probably the only thing a person needs for that moment. A few minutes of empathic listening could change the course of action of a person drastically, especially if it comes from the heart. I empathised with Aaryan's mother, not just as a formality, but with a genuine desire to help her. I listened not just to her words but also to the emotions embedded in them, trying to understand the situation as best

I could. I prayed intensely for some ideas to pop up for a probable solution.

"Can you bring your husband to meet me?" I asked. "I would like to talk to him."

She replied that her husband did not step out of the house. I suggested visiting her at their residence and meeting him there instead. She said she would confirm after talking to her husband. As our conversation continued, she opened up about her family and childhood. She shared how much she missed her father, whom she lost at nine.

"If my father were alive today, he would be the only person who would have heard me with so much patience and attention without judging," she spoke wistfully.

I felt uncomfortable and shy to hear such unexpected remarks for being considerably younger than her. I assured her that I feel honoured to support my students in any way I can. "To *me*, they are more than a family," I added.

As she was about to depart, I shared some wise words that a dear friend told me many years ago: *Whenever you go through a harrowing situation in life, don't panic. Try to tolerate it. For sure, like everything else, it will come to pass.*

I did visit Aaryan and his parents at their residence a few days later. When I entered, Aaryan took special pride in introducing me to his father. In stark contrast to my imagination, I found his father gentlemanly and cordial. I spent considerable time with the family, explaining simple concepts of mindful living. I taught them some prayers and meditation techniques that they could start with.

Rather than discussing the issue at hand, I instead sought to equip Aaryan's father with elements of living rooted in the mode of goodness. I felt him to be a victim of circumstances. He was probably aware of the gravity of the situation but could not extricate himself from this quagmire on his own.

We met a few more times subsequently. It took a few weeks for the changes to be evident in Aaryan's father. Slowly but steadily, he was inching towards a normal lifestyle. In this case, the good thing was that he was willing to change; however, he needed the support of someone he could trust.

It struck me that this case was a perfect example of negative mindfulness. Aaryan's father had given himself fully to the online game he was addicted to, being completely oblivious to anything else in the world. Technically speaking, he was mindful, but in the wrong way. Under the influence of the mode of ignorance, a person, out of illusion, takes misery to happiness. Such was the condition of Aaryan's father. However, he needed to escape the fantasy realm to understand that he had multiple responsibilities to take care of: his career, family, health and future.

In all such cases, the solution is to gradually raise the person to the platform of the mode of goodness by introducing them to a lifestyle that fosters it. Such a lifestyle helps people connect to their inner self, thus making them feel deep, satisfying and enduring happiness. The only *prerequisite* here is a little willingness to make the change.

# 10

# *Stages of a Meditative Yoga*

## A small boy's crisis

In the Vedas is a story of a five-year-old boy, Dhruva, who faced an identity crisis. Dhruva's father, Uttanpada, was a King. One day, while Dhruva attempted to sit on his father's lap, he was forcibly dragged down by his stepmother, Suruchi, for her son, Uttama, to sit comfortably on the King's lap. Despite being almost the same age as Uttama, Suruchi feared Dhruva would become the future King since he was the son of the eldest queen, Suniti.

Suruchi chastised Dhruva with many hurtful words, saying he was not qualified to sit on the King's lap because he was not born of her. Her words enraged Dhruva beyond the limit, who, with a face red in anger, looked to his father for justice. However, King Uttanpada refrained from intervening due to his concern about displeasing Suruchi, his favoured queen.

Feeling desolate, Dhruva ran to his own mother, Queen Suniti, seeking refuge. The palace attendants had already informed her of the incident.

Lifting her bitterly crying son onto her lap, Suniti spoke, "My dear Dhruva, *don't* wish anything inauspicious for others. Anyone who inflicts pain upon others will inevitably feel the same pain themselves. Your father does not consider me his queen and leaves me in neglect. He is too ashamed to acknowledge me."

Composing herself a bit, she spoke to him with kindness, "My dear Dhruva, the love and affection you yearn from your father, and even from me, is incomparable to the boundless love that the *Supreme One* has for you."

When Dhruva inquired about how he could reach the *Supreme One*, his mother replied, "I have heard sages realise Him within themselves by controlling the mind and regulating life air through the practice of *Dhyana yoga.* I don't know of any other means to mitigate your suffering."

Fixed in his determination to practice Dhyana yoga, Dhruva left home for the forest. But he needed guidance on how to do it. While on his way, he met the celestial sage Narada, who initially discouraged Dhruva from going into the forest and advised him to return home. However, seeing Dhruva's unwavering determination, Narada provided him with detailed guidance on how to practise Dhyana yoga, the culmination of which is the realisation of the Supreme One within.

Following is a description of the process of Dhyana yoga, which Dhruva practised in the forest. This process can be broken down into eight steps, known as Astanga yoga. Asta means 'eight,' and anga means 'limbs,' referring to the eight steps involved.

The eight steps of Dhyana yoga are as follows:

### 1. Yama

This stage involves reining our gross senses from any sense object considered improper.

### 2. Niyam

After reining the senses, they need to be given proper engagement. This stage is called Niyam. For instance, following Yama would restrain our eyes from seeing anything improper, whereas Niyam would dictate how to engage our eyes in seeing something good or acceptable.

The same holds true about engaging all our knowledge-acquiring and working senses.

The Yam and Niyam principles are akin to preparing the soil before sowing seeds to promote proper germination and growth. Similarly, only after mastering Yam and Niyam can the subsequent stages of Dhyana yoga be realised.

There are four pillars sustaining humanity. These are cleanliness, austerity, mercy, and truthfulness. Following the principles of Yam and Niyam enables us to adhere to these principles efficiently.

The first pillar, maintaining cleanliness, is essential—both externally and internally. Keeping ourselves and our surroundings clean through regular bathing and hygiene practices is important for maintaining external cleanliness. However, the focus should be more on cultivating a clean and pure mind, reflected in our words and actions. True cleanliness begins from within and extends outwardly to create a healthy and harmonious environment. When one's mind is under control and guided by proper intelligence, it naturally leads to appropriate speech and action. Maintaining trustworthiness in relationships is also a vital aspect of being internally clean.

Austerity can be defined as the willingness to endure temporary difficulties to achieve something higher. For a farmer, this might mean toiling in the field, enduring cold, heat, or rain. For a student, austerity might mean dedicating time and energy to studying. Raising children responsibly is austerity on the part of parents.

Austerity involves three essential qualities: enthusiasm, determination, and patience. Taking any intoxication, like alcohol, cigarettes, drugs, etc., significantly hinders our ability to practice austerity. It makes the addicted person lose enthusiasm to initiate anything worthwhile, or even if they manage to start a task, they won't find sufficient determination and patience needed to see it through to completion.

Mercy is the third pillar of humanity. It means not giving pain to anyone through our gestures, words, or actions. Some people are merciful to humans but not to animals. Some are merciful towards animals but not to humans. One needs to be mindful to be gracious to both. Truthfulness is the fourth pillar, which encompasses aligning our thoughts, words, intentions, and actions. Not distorting the truth is also a part of it. Engaging in any form of gambling compromises our ability to remain truthful.

Following the above principles of cleanliness, mercy, austerity, and truthfulness brings a person nearer to the mode of goodness. And as a natural consequence, one becomes more mindful in every aspect of life, including eating, sleeping, relationships, recreation, and communication.

### 3. Asana

Asana, the third stage of Dhyana yoga, denotes a specific bodily posture. The various yoga practices comprise a vast array of Asanas, each with a unique posture. These can include seating, standing, and lying positions, as well as twisting and bending movements or a combination of several.

When practising yoga, it's required to pair each Asana with a specific breathing exercise to maintain an optimum balance between the body and mind. However, among all the Asanas, only those that keep the spine straight qualify for meditation purposes. With practice, one can learn to maintain a meditative posture for an extended period without bodily movement.

A simple and fundamental form of meditative Asana that anyone can practice involves sitting cross-legged on a mat with a straight neck and head, hands resting on the knees, and eyes closed.

Achieving a certain level of proficiency in Asana is a prerequisite for effectively practising Pranayam, the next stage of Dhyana yoga.

### 4. Pranayam

Prana vayu, or life air, is the energy that sustains the entire body. It consists of ten different forms, five of which are major and five minor. Together, they work to keep our whole body functioning properly. A few of these life airs are gross, while most are a subtle manifestation of air. On a subtler level, these life airs influence and, in turn, get influenced by our mind and consciousness.

Pranayam is an extended version of mindful breathing that aims to establish a harmonious balance of the ten prana vayus within us. It helps a practitioner attain a sound state of body and mind, which is required to practice Dhyana yoga effectively.

The five major prana vayus are: Prana, Apana, Samana, Udana and Vyana.

### Prana:

The first prana vayu is named Prana itself. It enables us to inhale, exhale, and swallow food, thereby providing strength to the body through these activities. Thus, it is called Prana, which means the life force. Prana is generated in the chest area. The practice of Pranayam raises the level of prana within us, thus ensuring purer qualities of the heart, such as strength and courage. Interestingly, among all the life air we have, 'Prana' is the only one we can directly control.

### Apana:

The Apana air expels waste and bodily fluids such as faeces, foul air from the rectum, urine, semen, and ova. Additionally, it is crucial in nourishing the fetus during pregnancy and facilitating its expulsion through the uterus at birth.

### Samana:

Samana is the air that mingles with the foodstuff in the stomach and sometimes comes out through the mouth in the form of belching. It is responsible for maintaining a proper digestive fire in the belly, called *jatharagni*, by activating the digestive organs and their secretions. In addition to helping digest the food, Samana also serves as a distributor, sending the assimilated energy from the food to various parts of the body. It is generated in the navel. Prana and Apana are two opposing forces. Samana helps in striking a balance between the two.

If Samana becomes weak, despite taking an adequately nutritious diet, we will not get proper nourishment because of poor assimilation of the nutrients.

### Udana:

Udana coordinates and controls the movements of the legs, arms, and neck. It directs the activities of the brain, our five sensory organs, and our ability to communicate through speech. Irregular udana causes inefficiency in physical and mental work and an inability to think or express oneself adequately.

### Vyana:

Vyana works as a complement to all major and minor pranas, ensuring their proper functioning. Positioned as the body's energy reservoir, it pervades the entire body and replenishes all other pranas with extra power whenever they need it. Vyana regulates and coordinates all muscular movements and is also responsible for the flow of perspiration and the appearance of goosebumps.

In addition to the five major pranas, there exist five forms of minor pranas which assist the functioning of the major pranas. All minor pranas derive their energy from Udana and are more subtle in nature than the aforementioned major pranas.

The five minor pranas are as follows:

### Naga:

When the air element in the stomach is agitated, Naga becomes active and tries to throw the agitated air out of the stomach. Naga remains inactive as long as diet and digestion are healthy. In the state of perfect meditation, Naga does not function.

### Koorma:

This vayu is responsible for blinking the eyes, which is vital for keeping them healthy and moist. The eyes shine due to the energy of Koorma. Although Koorma operates in a small area, it has much force, and during meditation, it helps to enhance concentration, making it more firm and deep.

### Krikara:

This vayu causes yawning, hunger, and thirst and assists in respiration. The control of Krikara is especially helpful during fasting and meditation. With proper practice, when Krikara is controlled, laziness, sleep, hunger, and thirst are overcome.

### Devadatta:

This vayu causes sneezing and also aids in respiration. It gets triggered by sharp or irritating smells and causes pain in the nostrils.

Dhananjaya:

This vayu pervades the entire body and is closely connected to the organ of touch, the skin. It governs the functioning of the muscles, arteries, veins, and skin. The swelling experienced during an injury is due to the motion of Dhananjaya. It is the last prana to leave the body after death, and its absence is responsible for the decomposition of the body.

Although the ten major and minor pranas are identified individually, they work together synchronously. For instance, in the process of eating, Prana assists in swallowing the food, Samana facilitates digestion and supports the assimilation of the energy from the food, Vyana preserves this energy and distributes it throughout the body, Apana eliminates the waste material, and Udana harnesses the energy derived from the food for both physical and mental work.

## Controlling our breathing

Among all the vayus or life airs, we only have direct control over the first life air, Prana vayu. By regulating this air through proper breathing exercises in combination with suitable asanas, it is indeed possible to achieve a state of balance for all the pranas, ensuring an optimised harmony between body and mind.

Taking in the air is known as purak, and it should be done slowly, filling the lungs. Holding the air inside comfortably for as long as possible is referred to as antar, i.e. internal kumbhak, during which our body absorbs energy from the air. Exhaling slowly is called rechak. The next step is to pause before taking in the next breath. This pause action is called baahya, i.e. external kumbhak. Through regular practice, one can increase the duration of purak, rechak, and kumbhak.

In an advanced stage of meditation, a person can suspend breathing for a prolonged duration, keeping their mind entirely focused on their desired object of meditation. However, to start with, a simple mindful breathing exercise we introduced earlier can easily be practised by everyone. This is also a form of Pranayam and has many benefits. During mindful breathing, ideally, the duration of purak should be equal to the duration of rechak, and the duration of antar kumbhak should be equal to that of baahya kumbhak.

## 5. Pratyahar

In Dhyana yoga, Pratyahar is the step that involves clearing the mind of negative thoughts to make room for positive ones. However, it can only be achieved after successfully completing the initial steps of Yam, Niyam, Asana, and Pranayam.

The final four steps of Dhyana yoga, starting with Pratyahar and progressing to Dharan, Dhyana, and Samadhi, are increasingly advanced stages of concentration that enable one to focus their mind on desired objectives.

## 6. Dharan

The term "Dharan" denotes the act of holding something, in this context, holding something in the mind. At the stage of Dharan, an individual must accept thoughts that will lead them towards their desired goal of achieving inner happiness, contentment, and enlightenment. The previous step, Pratyahar, was all about emptying the bowl of the mind of any evil thoughts. However, it's equally important to fill the mind with positive thoughts; this is where the practice of "Pratyahar" and "Dharan" go hand in hand. It's like preparing a piece of land for farming; you must till the soil and remove the weeds before you can sow the seeds. Similarly, "Pratyahar" is incomplete without the addition of positive thoughts, or else the mind will drift back to its lower nature.

To achieve this, we must give the mind a taste of something higher. Replace the bitterness of anger with the sweetness of love, the despair of hopelessness with the optimism of hope, the darkness of ignorance with the light of knowledge, and the harshness of violence with the tenderness of mercy. Replace sluggishness with a sense of purpose and fickleness with steadfastness. Let ignorance dissipate in the face of goodness. Just imagine how wonderful it would be to possess such divine qualities!

Our associations have a profound impact on who we become. Surround ourselves with people who possess such qualities and read and hear about them. Having an ideal to aspire to is vital in life. The first step towards achieving this is developing a strong determination. Once we have a firm resolve, we can stick to a set path towards the goal and achieve it within a short time. As one's belief system is, so shall they become—this is Dharan.

Even at the level of Dharan, some taint in consciousness may persist, much like a fan that takes a while to come to a complete stop after being turned off. Yama, Niyam, and other earlier stages of Dhyana yoga are analogous to cutting off the power supply to a running fan. Dharan can be associated with a slowing-down fan. The residual remnants of our darker tendencies might surface even during the Dharan stage; however, even with these minor imperfections, our inner nature doesn't limit us from realising that our true self, the 'soul', essentially is enriched with divine qualities, which temporarily has got covered over.

## 7. Dhyana

The next stage of Dhyana yoga is simply known as *Dhyana*. It is the ability to concentrate our mind on our desired goal. Just as a potter must knead the mud to make it soft before shaping it, our minds can only be moulded into Dhyana after successfully navigating all the previous stages of yoga. There is a story of an arrow-maker who was so engrossed in honing his arrow that he failed to take notice of the pompous entourage of the king passing by. This shows the perfection of Dhyana or mental concentration, where a person becomes oblivious to everything except his desired object of meditation.

## 8. Samadhi

Samadhi is the culmination of Dhyana yoga. It is a stage where the physical body is awake, but the mind, with all its capriciousness, enters a state of dormancy. Consciousness attains a level of pure goodness, being entirely freed from passion and ignorance.

Let's explore the concept of Kosh in our body to better understand the stage of Samadhi.

**Kosh:**

Every human being has five layers of coverings, known as kosh. Some of these layers are gross, while others are subtle in nature.

The first level or layer of covering consists of our gross body, also called annamaya kosh. The term anna means 'food', maya means 'composed of', and 'kosh' means covering. Our gross body requires food for sustenance; thus, it is named the 'annamaya kosh' of our existence. Annamaya kosh consists of earth, water, fire, air, and ether. After death, these five elements merge into their respective parts in Nature.

This body's next level of covering is known as the pranamaya kosh, which encompasses our working senses and prana vayus (life airs). Pranamaya kosh is subtler than the annamaya kosh, representing the energy level inside us. It pervades and supports our physical body and is also referred to as the pranic aspect of our being. Together, the annamaya and pranamaya kosh make up the fundamental framework of our human structure.

> The third layer in the human body is the manomaya kosh. It consists of knowledge-acquiring senses along with mind and intelligence. This holds annamaya and pranamaya kosh together as an integrated unit.
>
> Vigyanamaya kosh is the fourth layer, which indicates the realisation of 'I' ness or the true identity of ourselves. A person in such a consciousness is less plagued by the excessive demands of the body, mind, and senses, understanding that as a spirit soul, they are superior to both gross and subtle bodies.

Imagine a scenario where a group of children are playing cricket near your home. Suddenly, you hear a loud crash—the sound of a cricket ball colliding with your parked car's windshield. You rush outside to see what has happened and are met with the sight of a shattered windshield.

If you strongly identify with your physical body, the annamaya kosh, you might feel like your heart has shattered instead of just the windshield. If your consciousness is primarily rooted in the pranamaya kosh, you may be inclined to start a physical altercation. As for those whose consciousness is rooted primarily in the manomaya kosh, you might analyse the situation like a philosopher or thinker would.

However, if your consciousness is rooted in the vigyanamaya kosh, you understand that although the car is separate from you, it is your responsibility to take care of it. While you may still feel some pain, it won't be to the same extent as those whose consciousness is rooted in lesser koshas, while your intelligence and mind remain clear about the next course of action.

Feeling a certain level of attachment to our physical body and the people and things associated with it is an essential aspect of our everyday functioning in this world. A mother feels attached to her child based on love and affection. We feel connected to the place of our birth based on a sense of gratitude, duty, and love. We feel a special attachment to things that belong to us.

Similarly, attachment to our body motivates us to take necessary precautions to protect ourselves from harm, often based on a healthy sense of fear. For instance, we exercise caution when crossing the road or dealing with fire and electricity to ensure our physical safety.

Attachments can't be nullified intrinsically, but those whose consciousness is primarily rooted in the vigyanamaya kosh can give a proper meaning to them. They remain conscious that though their real self, the soul, is beyond the body, they are responsible for taking proper care of annamaya, pranamaya, and manomaya koshas. They recognise that their body, both gross and subtle, is a prime vehicle for action.

> The fifth and final sheath of our being is known as anandamaya kosh. This layer is where we come to realise that our true self, the soul, is part and parcel of one Supreme whose consciousness pervades and supports the entire universe. Just like a spoonful of seawater has all the qualities

of the sea, we, as part of the Supreme, possess all his divine attributes, albeit in a minute quantity.

Those who have identified with anandamaya kosh have reached the stage of Samadhi. They have evolved to a realm where all their experiences are spiritual in nature. Correct practice of Dhyana yoga gradually raises one from their bodily consciousness, known as annamaya kosh, to the stage of ultimate bliss, known as anandamaya kosh.

## Dhruva achieves perfection

After taking leave from sage Narada, Dhruva embarked on a journey through the wilderness, traversing several days until he arrived at a secluded forest on the banks of the Yamuna River. There, he bathed in the river and quenched his thirst with its invigorating flow. He began practising the control of his senses, commencing with following the principles of Yam and Niyam.

In the first month, Dhruva ate only fruits and berries every third day, only to keep his body and soul together; following the teachings of Narada, Dhruva diligently practised Asana and Pranayam, always holding the form of the Supreme within his heart as his desired object of meditation while repeatedly uttering the divine chant, *Om namo bhagvate Vasudevaya*, the mantra imparted to him by sage Narad.

In the second month, Dhruva heightened his austerity by subsisting only on dry grass and leaves every six days. By the third month, he surpassed even that level of self-deprivation by fasting completely and drinking only water every ninth day. In the fourth month, Dhruva managed to survive by inhaling air only once every twelfth day.

The fifth month saw him master Pranayam so perfectly that he could suspend his breath and stand on one leg (Fig. 10.1) like a motionless column while chanting the mantra within with complete concentration.

*Fig. 10.1. Meditative pose of Dhruva*

At the culmination of his rigorous practice, at the end of the sixth month, Dhruva finally achieved the stage of Samadhi, where he realised his oneness in purpose with the Supreme Self. He began to feel a deep affection for all beings, and in turn, he also experienced a love a million times greater than what he sought from his father, mother, or anyone else. *All* the feelings of anger, grudges, and resentment he had held towards his father and stepmother vanished completely. This benevolence towards one and all is the gift of Samadhi that Dhruva had attained.

Upon returning home, Dhruva discovered that the whole kingdom had been lamenting for him during his absence, including his father, King Uttanpada. Even Suruchi, his stepmother, who had spoken so harshly at the spur of the moment, *genuinely* repented for her unmindful words and actions that led to Dhruva's leaving the palace.

When Dhruva was a certain age, his father appointed him king, and he retired to the forest to practice Dhyana yoga himself. Dhruva remained in a state of Samadhi throughout his life, even while performing his kingly duties. All his activities were acts performed under Samadhi.

Samadhi is the pinnacle of spiritual enlightenment that anyone can experience in this world, a state of being where one experiences perfect bliss, peace, and mercy towards all. A person in this state derives their strength and purpose from the truth itself, dedicating themselves to the welfare of others and always behaving in a way that is pleasing to all—free from any desire to be falsely honoured, such a person remains focused on the execution of his duties.

The initial stages of Dhyana yoga are more or less a practice of restraining the senses, while the intermediate stages focus on controlling and engaging the mind. Finally, in the state of Samadhi, one can engage their senses and mind in any activity with total concentration. All their work becomes an act of selfless sacrifice. This is known as active Samadhi. At this point, a person has been able to strike the perfect balance of all five koshas.

There is a dire need for everyone to connect first to their inner self and then subsequently transcend to connect to the Super Self. Such a person, who is filled *inside*, does not hanker for the need to get satisfied by something external. Without this inner connection, dissatisfaction and hankering will always linger in the person's heart, leaving them to wonder, "*Why* am I still not happy even after achieving everything I once dreamed of?"

Mindfulness practices gradually raise our consciousness in a way that creates better harmony between all the koshas. Certainly, it may not be feasible for us to go through rigorous practices to reach the perfect stage of Samadhi, which Dhruva had achieved in just six months. However, the more we elevate our consciousness by practising different steps of Dhyana yoga, the more bliss and satisfaction we will experience. In more practical terms, with a little endeavour, everyone can reasonably and efficiently practice at least some of the steps of—Asana, Pranayam, and Meditation—with significant benefits derived from it.

# 11

# *Mindful Healing*

## Self-healing through conscious awareness

Whenever we experience an injury or acute pain in any part of our body, our attention naturally shifts to that area, even if only temporarily. This response triggers a self-healing process within the body, where a surge of energy is directed towards the affected area, revitalising the pranamaya kosh, the energy level in that part of the body.

The same principle is involved in mindful healing, where one can channel the flow of *prana vayu* (life air) to a particular body part by passing a conscious awareness to it through mindful breathing. This energises the pranamaya kosh in that area and thus primes it to self-heal from any pain or discomfort whatsoever.

In essence, "Energy flows where the attention goes" is the working principle behind mindful healing.

One can practice mindful healing not only for a specific area of the body but for the whole body as well. The process involves dividing the body into distinct elements and then consciously passing awareness through each one, thereby energising the pranamaya kosh in that part. The entire process typically takes around 15–20 minutes to complete smoothly, so it's best to schedule it when you have some free time.

To begin your healing process, you can start with a simple Asana sitting on a chair with your palms resting on your knees. Ensure that you're comfortable. Release any stiffness in your body that you may notice firsthand. You can let your back comfortably rest against the chair's backrest for support.

Alternatively, you can opt for a sleeping Asana (Shavasana), where you lie down on a mat on the floor, looking upward, with your back resting against the ground. Keep your hands on the sides, stretch your legs, and relax. If being quickly induced into sleep due to the relaxing experience of healing is the goal, then adopting this posture is a recommended one. However, it may not complete the entire process of full-body healing.

Irrespective of the Asana you choose, first bring awareness to your breath with a few deep mindful inhalations and exhalations, then proceed with the steps as described. Eyes can be either open or closed.

The entire process has to be carried out slowly and smoothly, giving sufficient time to each body part.

1. Take a moment to shift attention to your left foot while breathing slowly, deeply and mindfully. Pay attention to any sensations of pain or discomfort by gently shifting your awareness across the sole, heel, ankle, toes, and the top surface of the foot. With each breath, energise different elements in this body part. Visualise how your breath, in combination with other types of life air, gives rise to the agility in that foot. Keep in mind that our attempt is just to energise the pranamaya kosh in this specific region. What actually will heal this part for any pain or discomfort is the body itself.

For each part of your body, follow the three-step process of PIE:

P- Pass conscious awareness on a specific body part.

I- Investigate all the elements in that body part and observe whether there is any pain or discomfort.

E- Energise that part with a few slow and deep mindful breathing while keeping the awareness fixed on this part.

2. Next, carry out the three-step PIE protocol for each section of the right foot.

P- Pass conscious awareness to the right foot.

I- Investigate if there is any pain or discomfort in the sole, heel, ankle, toes, and the upper surface of the right foot.

E- Energise different parts of the right foot with a few slow and deep mindful breaths while keeping the awareness fixed on this region.

3. Following this, proceed to apply the same three-step PIE process for the remaining parts of the body—Left leg, right leg, left knee, right knee, left thigh, right thigh, pelvic region, lower abdomen, lower back, upper abdomen and upper back, chest, left hand, right hand, left elbow, right elbow, left arm, right arm, left shoulder, right shoulder, neck, and face. Slowly move upwards from the feet to the head while maintaining a mindful approach.

Finally, perform the three-step PIE process for your head as follows:

- P- Pass conscious awareness to different portions of your head.
- I- Check for any pain or discomfort in your forehead, as well as the back, top, and sides of your head. The skull houses the brain, an extremely complicated organ of various neural tissues that help coordinate different bodily functions. Observe if there is any stress at this level.
- E- Energise different portions of your head, including the brain, with slow and deep mindful breaths while keeping awareness fixed in this region.

Finally, extend your awareness across the entire body, carefully noting any sensations of relaxation. With this, you have successfully completed the process of mindful healing for your entire body. This comprehensive approach to mindful healing can be immensely beneficial in high-pressure situations, such as in academic or professional settings where stress and anxiety can be commonplace, leading to an overall improvement in well-being.

# 12

# *Sutras for Mindful Parenting*

## Pass on the baton

Once, I witnessed a group of black ants patrolling down the centre of my room in the monastery, struggling to carry a dead insect. In the beginning, five ants took the load, with a few others moving ahead or behind them in the line. After a few seconds, two ants from the original group left to move up in the line. With only three ants left, the weight became increasingly difficult for them to bear. But soon, three more ants from behind came to their aid, bringing the total count to six. Shortly after, one more ant from the group left to move forward, and a few more from behind eventually joined in the effort.

The count kept changing, and the original group had been entirely replaced by the time the dead insect was successfully transported to its supposed destination. It made me wonder who the project belonged to. Was it the ants who initiated it, the ones who contributed in between, or the ones who ultimately completed it?

As I pondered, it dawned on me that the project was a product of teamwork. At least with this particular group of ants, Nature had awarded them an in-built system of coordination to do their part and pass on the baton to the next ones. It left me to reason, as a human being, isn't this supposed to be how mindfully we should hand down a good value system to the next generation?

The concepts explored in this chapter are meant not only for parents but everyone because, in one way or another, each of us is involved in inspiring and guiding children and their families. Parents and grandparents have their respective roles to play, as do neighbours, friends, teachers, and society as a whole, all of them influencing a child's successful upbringing. Even as a monk, I feel blessed to have had this opportunity, for so many years, to closely guide children, parents, and guardians towards a wholesome way of life.

Raising children can be a complex undertaking, but there are some essential principles that, if followed mindfully, could make the experience easier and more meaningful. This chapter delves into these principles and explores how they can be applied to parenting.

## Begin with a goal in mind

"What do you mean by the success of a child?" I was asked by the father of one of my students during a question-answer session at a parenting workshop.

Without a second thought, I responded, "A successful child is one who is a happy and healthy individual, rooted in good values, and has healthy self-esteem."

"What about their education and career?" another parent chimed in.

"Education has three components: knowledge, skill, and values," I clarified. "A supportive culture, favourable atmosphere at home, nurturing good values, regulating eating and recreational activities and like will keep children physically healthy and emotionally happy. And as a natural upshot, as children grow, they will inevitably be inspired to acquire age-appropriate knowledge and skills, too. Our role should be to provide a favourable support system for them. However, only setting their career path right as a prime goal might leave you with a child whose internal growth is not being properly taken care of."

To further elucidate the point, I posed the question, "Can a tall building stand without a strong foundation?"

As expected, the answer was a definite "No."

I went on to explain, "People often discuss and even travel across countries to witness some of the tallest buildings on the planet. In general, what everyone admires in a structure is only the visible part of it. However, what they fail to recognise is the effort and care that goes into creating a solid foundation, the very thing that allows the building to stand tall.

"Likewise, success in one's career, fame, financial stability, and the like are comparable to the visible part of a building that can't stand strong without a solid foundation.

This foundation is compared to an individual's physical and emotional well-being. Without a strong base, even the slightest disturbance in life can cause the entire structure of external success, which people usually adore in us, to crumble. Work more upon the internal growth of the child, the unseen part, the foundation of the building. And rest assured that as they mature, material success will naturally follow them."

## Understand your child first

In *Niti Shastra*, Chanakya has succinctly divided a child's development into four distinct age groups, understanding which will give one a fair idea about age-appropriate parenting techniques to be adopted.

The first phase, *Kaumara*, spans from birth to five years. During this time, children require an abundance of love and affection from their parents. Children in this age group perceive themselves as the exclusive object of everyone's love and attention.

The next five years, age six to ten, is known as *Pauganda*. As children make the transition from *Kaumara* to *Pauganda*, they begin to comprehend that society consists of more than just themselves. They desire to establish relationships with others, particularly in forming friendships. At this point, parents must instil basic socialisation skills in their children.

The next five years, age 11–15, is known as *Kaishora*, the pre-and early-teen years of a child's life. At this age, children develop an attraction for adventure, thrill, and the opposite sex due to hormonal changes in the body. Control of the senses and discipline needs to be instilled in them, training for which should ideally begin around the middle or end of *Pauganda* age. As children reach the age of 15 and beyond, known as *Yauvana*, parents should strive to be more of a friend to their grown-up children. Potentially, grown-up children are the best friends of their parents.

Thus, depending on the age group, first, understand your child's psychology properly and then, keeping the end goal in mind, apply the following sutras for balanced parenting. In essence, the various principles discussed in this chapter are detailed applications of mindfulness practices discussed earlier in this book.

## Sutra 1: Spend quality time with your child

### Hearing the unheard

I reached out to Rishi, Keshav's father, as I was curious to know why Keshav wasn't able to attend my last class. Keshav was in grade IV then and was part of my weekly class on Value Education.

Rishi explained that Keshav had a sports day event at school, which ran late. I told him to bring Keshav the following evening to cover the missed session. As agreed, Rishi dropped Keshav at my office the next day. As usual, whenever Keshav would meet me, he first showed me his homemade DIY science gadgets, his hobby. As Keshav described his latest self-made devices, I marvelled at the scientific genius he was exhibiting at this age.

It took me some time before I could move on to the worksheets of the last class on 'how to develop good association'. We sat on the mat, and I explained the lesson and related activities to Keshav. The individual session lasted for around half an hour, after which I conversed informally with Keshav, inquiring about his life in general while waiting for his father to pick him up.

During our conversation, I asked Keshav who his closest friend was, to which he immediately responded, "It's Aman."

"Does he study in the same school?" I asked.

"*Yes*, we are classmates," Keshav confirmed with pride.

Curious about Keshav's social circle, I asked him to tell me more about his friends and what he appreciated about each of them. He jovially went on speaking for a while, but his demeanour shifted when he mentioned Mayank. With a tinge of hostility in his tone, he stated, "I *hate* him."

"Who is Mayank?" I asked.

'I hate him' was the only disdainful reply from Keshav, revealing a mix of anger, resentment, and powerlessness written across his face.

It took a while for Keshav to recover and for me to attempt to communicate with him and try to understand what was going on in his mind. As we conversed, the complete story unfolded.

Keshav, a soft-spoken boy, was a serious victim of bullying by Mayank, who was one year senior in the school. Both shared the same school bus. Mayank would make sure to sit near Keshav to make fun of him all throughout by abusing him verbally or physically. Mayank also used to give his writing assignments to Keshav, who felt pressured to complete them by the next day. Keshav dreaded going to school because of the bus ride.

"How long has it been?" I asked.

"Over two months now," Keshav replied.

I inquired if Keshav had informed his parents about the issue.

"*Yeah*, I talked to my mom," he responded.

"And did she take any action?" I probed further.

"She told me to learn to adapt," Keshav murmured. Probably his mother couldn't comprehend the gravity of the situation. Shortly thereafter, his father arrived to pick him up.

"Who is Keshav's closest friend?" I asked Rishi. Fortunately, he got it right. "Aman," He replied.

"Do you know Mayank?" I further asked. Rishi didn't seem to be familiar with Mayank, and he couldn't initially figure out why I was interested in this boy. I recounted the entire story to Rishi, who till now was completely unaware of this problem in his son's life. Perhaps after a cold response from his mother, Keshav lacked the courage to discuss it with his father. Rishi promised to look into the matter after talking to Keshav's mother.

The next day, both parents met with the school Principal, and after a detailed investigation, Keshav's disclosure about Mayank was found to be true. The Principal took prompt action. She changed thc school bus for Keshav and gave a stern warning to Mayank to mend his behaviour. Witnessing the support of those around him made Keshav feel safe and immensely relieved.

When interacting with children, it's crucial to pay attention not only to what they say aloud but also to their unspoken words, emotions, and concealed feelings. Nowadays, Bullying, like what Keshav went through, is a widespread problem in schools. Therefore all parent must equip their children to handle it properly. It is essential to explain to children what bullying is and isn't.

Bullying is—

something that makes you feel bad or hurt.

something people do on purpose.

something hard for the person being bullied to stop.

something that happens more than once.

something that no one should be part of.

However, it is not considered bullying when—

friends are just playing, and everyone is okay with it.

equally matched kids fight.

someone makes fun of you once.

someone unintentionally makes you feel uncomfortable.

The following activity sheet is designed to help parents identify if their child is experiencing ongoing bullying.

The child should check off any boxes that apply to their experiences.

| Are you called mean names by other kids? | |
|---|---|

| | |
|---|---|
| Do other kids hit, kick, push, or punch you on purpose? | |
| Do kids leave you out of their groups purposely? | |
| Do other kids make fun of the way you look or do something? | |
| Is it hard for you to make friends? | |
| Are you sometimes afraid to go to school? | |
| Are you terrified of any particular kid in the school? | |
| Do other kids laugh when someone hurts you? | |

The following sheet assesses whether your child acts as a bully. Check the boxes next to anything that applies to you (To be filled by the child).

| | |
|---|---|
| Do you try to hurt other kids purposely? | |
| Do you tease other kids about how they look or behave? | |
| Are other kids afraid of you? | |
| Do you try to hurt kids, mostly when adults are not around? | |
| Do you take and break other kids' stuff? | |
| Do you think it is okay to hurt some people? | |
| Do you say mean things about others in person, on the phone, or online? | |

As a parent, it is important to understand that irrespective of the child's age; they will open up to reveal their heart only when there is a deep bond between you and them. This isn't something that can be achieved overnight—it requires a sustained investment in your relationship. If you are not confident that your child will feel comfortable opening up to you, consider enlisting the help of older siblings or someone else they trust and can confide in freely.

In my experience, I've found that children tend to reveal their hearts most readily when such activities are done as group work involving their peers. During a dedicated session on "How to deal with peer pressure and bullying," I was struck by how many children have experienced both being bullied and being bullies themselves at some point during their school years.

However, it's important to emphasise that just because others are engaging in bullying behaviour doesn't make it acceptable. We need to teach children to treat others as they themselves would like to be treated.

Reassure your child that being bullied is not their fault. Nobody deserves to be bullied, and your children are no exception. Encourage them to open up to trusted adults like teachers, parents, or older siblings if they ever feel like a victim. Remind them that they don't have to face this alone. If they ever feel like retaliating, stop them and impress firmly that this is not acceptable and should not be an option.

## What do children need the most?

As the adage goes, the most precious gift you can give to anyone, including your child, is your time. The initial step towards achieving this is by being physically present with your child. The next level involves spending quality time with your child, engaging in activities or interactions that they eagerly look forward to and that foster a deeper sense of belongingness in them.

For a child, a parent's physical presence is one of the most crucial needs, especially during the early years of childhood. It's irreplaceable, and nothing else can compare when it comes to making your child happy. And as a natural consequence of being emotionally satisfied and happy, a child develops robust physical immunity and thus falls sick less. Especial care needs to be taken in this regard when both parents are working.

When Ribhav was seven years old, he confided to his working mother that he didn't like being alone at home when she was not around. His mother shared the child's concerns with her husband when he returned home. The next day, they both sat down with Ribhav to discuss a solution. The mother promised to adjust her work schedule to be home more often, even though it would mean a reduction in her income. So, instead of costly vacations and other luxuries, the couple decided to manage with relatively less expensive holidays and simple living.

Ribhav's response brought tears to his mother's eyes: "You can cancel vacations, Mom. I need *you*, not the vacation."

Apparently, this feeling had been in Ribhav's heart since early childhood, but he didn't know how to express it then.

However, regardless of the fact that spending both quality and physical time with your children is a fundamental principle for all parents, the practical consideration as to how this could be achieved can vary widely in each case. With some deliberation on the guidelines outlined in this chapter, parents should be able to work out a model that best suits them.

A very effective way of spending quality time with children is to set the habit of having at least one meal together. As discussed earlier, meal times should not be used to correct children or discuss anything negative or controversial. Encourage happy conversations over the food. Having a relaxed meal together, free from distractions, brings family members closer and emphasises the feeling of being a unit.

Another effective way to spend quality time is by telling stories to children, especially at bedtime. The act of listening to a story is always captivating and can create a special bond between parents and children. This tradition has become almost extinct now; it needs to be revived and cherished once again.

Spend time talking to children about their daily lives and what's happening in general. Try to hear not only their spoken words but also the emotions embedded in them. In general, children love to talk and share their happy as well as difficult moments as long as they feel like they won't be judged. One should be mindful that the presence of parents during special events, such as sports day at school, makes children feel valued. Make it a *priority* to attend; your child will remember it throughout the year.

Other ways of spending quality time with children could be playing indoor or outdoor games together, going for walks, trekking, swimming, or any activity that your child looks forward to spending time with you.

## ACTIVITY TIME

If you feel you can spend more time with your child(ren) than you currently are, consider what steps you can take to make it a reality.

________________________________________

________________________________________

________________________________________

________________________________________

### Sutra 2: Nurture children's self-esteem

Self-esteem is having respect for yourself and your abilities. A child's self-esteem increases if he answers a difficult question in class or is invited to lead a group in school. Conversely, being ridiculed or bullied by friends will cause their self-esteem to plummet. Being reprimanded by parents or teachers can cause their self-esteem to fall briefly before it returns to the

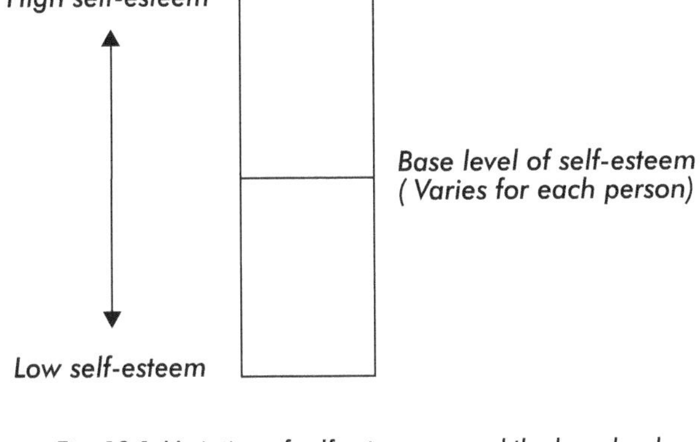


*Fig. 12.1. Variation of self-esteem around the base level*

individual's base level, which could be different for each child, depending on their upbringing.

However, prolonged exposure to a series of positive or negative influences can also cause the base level of an individual child's self-esteem to go up or down. As responsible parents or guardians, it is one's duty to maintain a positive and nurturing environment for the children, which eventually leads them to achieve healthy self-esteem.

## Be mindful; your words count

Analyse the following case:

Tara is a 13-year-old girl. She is getting dressed to attend a wedding with her parents.

Mom: Tara, come out fast. We are running late for the function.

Tara: Just one more minute, Mom.

After a while, Tara emerged from her room, wearing an outfit different from the new dress her mother had purchased for the occasion.

Mom (in disbelief and anger): *What* is this, Tara? You are supposed to wear the *new* dress.

Tara: But Mom, the new dress is a little tight for me.

Mom: But it looks better; go and change into it.

Tara: Please, Mom, this dress also looks good, and I am more comfortable wearing this.

After some back and forth, when the mother realised Tara would not agree to change, in frustration, she lashed out at her, "You are a constant headache for me, Tara. Better if a girl like you had not been born at all."

This made Tara burst into tears. She refused to go to the wedding, and the parents had to leave without her.

Think how Tara might have felt about the incident.

______________________________________________

______________________________________________

______________________________________________

______________________________________________

Did her mom really mean what she said? Probably not. On the spur-of-the-moment or out of a subconscious habit, she spoke something that negatively impacted Tara's self-esteem. A series of negative interactions like this would leave Tara feeling that she is not loved, or worse, she is not worthy of love.

Judge whether the following characterises a child with healthy or unhealthy self-esteem:

1. A child practices football every day to make his team win. ______________
2. Someone is confident of his team and does not even practice. ______________
3. A child does not want to play with his classmates because he thinks they are better than he is. ______________

## Be mindful of your child's potential

Aarav, a fourth-grade student, felt stressed due to the series of assignments and continuous tests common in many schools nowadays. I have known Aarav since he was a young child. He was a child who loved to talk and enquire about anything he observed. And he would only let you go if you satisfied his queries. Though intelligent, when it came to academics, he had developed a fear of studying over the years.

As the situation worsened, both parents decided to talk to the class teacher to check if there was any possibility of lightening the load for Aarav as he could not cope with the current evaluation system. As anticipated, the request was denied.

The only option left was to admit Aarav to some other school where he could easily cope. However, their decision was met with strong opposition from both relatives and friends who disapproved of the idea of sending Aarav to a school that was lesser known.

However, the parents remained firm in their decision. For them, Aarav's *natural* academic growth was more important than forced learning in a highly reputed school. The decision paid off as Aarav found the new school more comfortable and steadily improved academically.

Ideally, learning should be a fun experience for students and not some intimidating thing where constant pressure exists to perform and prove themselves. The objective of education should not solely be limited to producing toppers, as they will always be a small fraction of the student population. Every child is unique and has their own strength. Instead of trying to make them the 'best', we should try to bring out 'their personal best'. As a natural consequence of this approach, a child would grow up as a happy individual with healthy self-esteem. In this case, a timely and mindful analysis of the problem led Aarav's parents to find a solution where Aarav's needs for natural growth were met.

## Correcting children mindfully

If children make mistakes, tell them how to amend the error and make up for it. Give confidence to children that they won't be judged, yelled at, or punished if they make a mistake. Children can take risks if they know they have you to fall back on in case of trouble. Your words, tone and actions help your child understand whether they are worthwhile.

When correcting, don't compare them with other children. Don't nag at children, constantly reminding them of their mistakes. Target the issue at hand, not the person. By age 8 or 9, children develop enough conscience to understand where they went wrong. If you have a deep emotional bond with your child, it is possible to help them recognise their mistakes with a little effort. However, building such a connection requires investing a significant amount of quality time with your children.

Apart from correcting children, parents must also learn to offer genuine appreciation for anything good they observe in their child. Praise should be specific and sincere. Appreciate what good you see in them, how you feel about it, and sum up it in simple words.

### A child with healthy self-esteem will—

feel loved for who they are.
be able to have clear communication with parents/ guardians.
not be afraid of taking risks and trying new things.
be confident in a group.
be willing to help people.
possess the resilience necessary to bounce back from setbacks.
not hide things.
know what their strengths as well as weaknesses are.

## ACTIVITY TIME

Can you determine whether these statements would boost or damage a child's self-esteem? Put yourself in a child's shoes and consider how each statement might make you feel.

1. Your dad says, "Act your age."
2. A teacher says, "I expect more from someone your age."
3. A friend says, "I enjoy spending time with you."
4. Someone keeps telling you, "You're fat" or "You're skinny."

## Sutra 3: Be mindful not to overindulge your child

In recent years, a new approach to parenting has emerged where parents tend to cripple their children by constantly doing everything for them. This is called overindulgence. It's natural for parents to want their children to have a better life than they did. However, loving children doesn't mean showering them with everything they desire and letting them behave however they please. In fact, a too easy-going and carefree lifestyle tends to make children irresponsible.

Don't overindulge your child in the following ways:

### Buying too many things

It's possible that many parents were denied their childhood attractions, for example, new clothes, bicycles, computers or shoes. But now, with only one or two kids at home, parents have more resources and want to give their children what they may have missed out on.

Added to this is the shopping culture and consumerism, which might make you feel like you're not doing enough for your child unless you buy them everything they want or their friends have.

However, even if you have the means to purchase everything your child asks for, it's best not to do so. It can be challenging to determine how much is too much or too little for your child. Nonetheless, it's worth remembering that simplicity is a virtue that your child should learn from the start. Extravagance tends to undermine this.

Help your child realise that happiness lies not in possessing more but in meaningful things. One small thing loved can make a person happier than a ton of stuff.

## Not holding children accountable for their behaviour

During a casual conversation with my class, I asked if mobile phones were allowed in their schools.

"No," Amit, who was in grade eight then, spoke, "And not only that, there is a rule in our school that if you are caught with one, it would be confiscated for one month. After that, one of the parents has to visit the school to retrieve it personally. However, in most cases, parents don't turn up to collect the mobile. Instead, they opt to provide their child with a replacement phone."

It pained my heart to hear this. Parents should be mindful of the value system they want to instil in children. The irresponsible behaviour of children should not be rewarded. This type of parental behaviour leaves children with a 'who cares' attitude. If parents don't hold children accountable for small things, they won't hesitate to commit bigger crimes in the future. It's like teaching children that driving is all right when the traffic signal is red—which definitely is insane. Making children face the consequences of their inappropriate behaviour is, in fact, a sign of deeper love for them.

## Doing too much for them

It is crippling for a child when they get everything readymade. It is crucial that children, after the age of three or four years, start learning age-appropriate tasks such as brushing their teeth, bathing, feeding themselves, assisting with making their bed, tidying up their toys after playtime, watering plants, and more.

Can you think of age-appropriate tasks for your child?

________________________________________

________________________________________

________________________________________

It may appear to parents that small children are incapable of doing things, but that couldn't be further from the truth. Start early and small, understanding the child's ability. Also, check on what they agree to do. It should be a gradual transition rather than a forceful imposition on them.

Children can easily be inspired to help with chores provided they observe their parents themselves doing so. First, explain and demonstrate how a particular task should be done. Take the time to train them a few times. Be there to guide them and gradually delegate the responsibility as they become more confident. Do the same for other chores, including regular self-care tasks. Remain patient if the transition takes time. Every child is unique, and how quickly they learn can vary for each individual.

Benefits of doing chores—

It makes children feel part of the family.

It makes children learn self-reliance and teamwork.

It increases their self-esteem.

It inculcates in children the feeling that their effort contributes to the betterment of the whole—an attitude that makes them move beyond obedience to embrace responsibility for their actions.

### ACTIVITY TIME

**Determine whether the following actions exhibit obedience or responsibility:**

| | Obedient/ Responsible (select one) |
|---|---|
| Your daughter calls her grandmother and wishes her happy birthday without you telling her to do so. | |
| Your child practices on the keyboard only when you watch. | |
| Your child plays with her little sister only when told to do so. | |

## Sutra 4: Engage your children in healthy lifestyle choices

Ensuring the good physical health of a child is a vital aspect for any parenting technique to work successfully. A healthy body means a child who is not under or overweight, has good energy level and practices habits that promote well-being in areas such as diet, recreation, sleep, and overall engagement.

## Eating

Our physical and subtle consciousness are both directly impacted by the food we consume. The guidance we discussed in Chapter–8 on mindful eating, drinking, and sleeping is equally applicable to children as well.

Children have a good appetite; keeping this in mind, parents need to learn the art of preparing a fresh meal at home that is nutritious and tastes good. Choose foods that prominently fall under the "mode of goodness" as these types of foods aid in vitality, make one disease-free, and satisfy the mind. Special care must be taken to protect children from overconsumption of packaged ready-to-eat foods. While these types of foods may fill the belly and satisfy the taste buds, they ultimately lead to health hazards. The preservatives added to such foods make it difficult to digest them, leading to chronic diseases.

Food is a divine gift that Mother Nature gracefully has offered for our sustenance. It should never be used as a tool for punishment, such as depriving children of a meal for their mistakes.

## Recreation

It's important to encourage children to engage in physical play to prevent obesity. Ensure that children have the appropriate facility and time for this. Such physical engagement also helps them immensely in their emotional growth. Playing mobile and internet-based games seems appealing only until children don't get the delightful experience of physical outdoor activities such as kite flying, swimming, cycling, running, climbing and more. Such physical activities help children maintain proper height-to-weight ratio, build strength and flexibility, and assist in brain development.

Parents need to replace screen time with spending quality time with the family on a regular basis. This, in fact, is the biggest recreation for everyone in the family.

## Sutra 5: Be a role model yourself

Parents are the first and most spontaneous models for a child. The value system that parents exhibit in their own lives can reasonably be expected to get reflected in their children.

The following points will help to set a guideline in this regard:

As a parent, set an ideal example for children by showing how you honour and respect your spouse. A meaningful relationship makes one happy. Children should be able to see this in action, in a cordial relationship between parents. Children, even as young as four, can easily feel the warmth (or coldness) of the relationship between their parents, though they may not be able to articulate their observations until they reach a certain age.

Watching dissension between parents creates much emotional insecurity in the child. Any differences in opinion or conflicts between parents should be sorted out in seclusion and not in the child's visible or audible presence. Never try to garner the favour of your child to belittle your spouse. Both parents should sit together to come to a common parenting model, particularly regarding critical decisions about the child's life.

Encourage your children to embrace a life centred on serving and caring for others, including the older adults in the family. Involve your child with at least some philanthropic work. Inculcate a feeling in children that apart from them, there are others also in the society whom they need to take care of. Train children to share whatever little they can with others—humans and animals alike. Teach them charity and kindness through your own example. The idea should get across that this world is not a place only to receive but also to appropriately give back without being asked for.

Encourage your child to lead a regulated life by setting an example with your own lifestyle. This means demonstrating the mode of goodness through your eating habits, sleep routine, and leisure activities.

## ADDITIONAL TOPICS

### Dealing with sibling rivalry

"How do you stop fighting among siblings?" someone asked me during a parenting workshop.

To make the learning experiential, I asked everyone, "How many of you have siblings or cousins with whom you grew up together?"

Many raised their hands in affirmation.

To this, I asked, "How many of you had an issue with sibling fighting?" Almost everyone raised their hands again.

"How is your relationship with those siblings now? Do you miss them?" I probed.

With a *grin* on their faces, they nodded their heads in affirmation.

I continued, "The bond between siblings is one of the most enduring relationships a person can experience; only our siblings have seen us at our absolute worst and best. However, in my experience working with children, I have discovered that in most cases, sibling rivalry is both an unavoidable and an essential aspect of a child's emotional growth. At best, parents can endeavour to keep such rivalry within limits and be firm about setting boundaries—such as slang will not be tolerated."

## Care for the caregivers

One should understand that parents are not superhuman, nor is it expected of them. While parents try to offer their best to their children, there may be times when they fall short. As they grow up, children should learn that their caregivers must also be cared for.

Following is a personal account of a girl's life, in her own words, who experienced a very strained relationship with her father as she was growing up:

I did not have a perfect childhood. I was beaten up, screamed at, and cursed for anything my father perceived as wrong.

Once, when I refused to take it anymore, I told him that brute force would not make me respect him, let alone love him. He cried that night and never raised his hand to me again. His tears made me see a side of him that I never knew existed. He is only human, but what caused him to be this way? As I learned more about him from close relatives, I understood that his childhood wasn't easy either. It helped me empathise with him.

Though the physical assault stopped, the mental one continued. Life went on like this. In 2016, when I was 17, we had an argument, and we did not speak for months. It wasn't the first time, but this time it was different. It appeared that our mutual silence would continue eternally. During this time, I came across a youth workshop on 'caring for the caregivers'. I discovered that many ideal things could be expected from my father, but being human, he had limitations. I needed to play my part to mend this broken relationship, starting with the three-step process of S-E-C (Scan – Empathize – Choose). When I scanned my emotions toward my father, I discovered that more than hating him, I longed to be loved by him. However, the present scenario created a massive invisible wall between us. I acknowledged my hatred and empathised with my longing to be loved. As a solution, my facilitator at the workshop suggested I write a letter to my father expressing my gratitude towards him for everything I could think of. With much reluctance, I obliged. This is what I wrote and shared with my father:

*"My father may not be a hero, but he has done numerous things that make me proud to be his daughter. It is contradictory that he treated me like a son, from my boyish hairstyle to the red SPD jacket I wore on Children's Day in class two to how I look at life in general today. It has shaped me and made me who I am, not perfect, but striving to be at least half the man my dad is.*

*In a conservative patriarchal society, my father raised three daughters, never complained, loved us devotedly, and always gave us more than we ever wanted. He has gone through many things to become who he is today, that too without any support or siblings to help him out. He put his health at risk to give his family everything we would ever want and more.*

*Being down to earth and having empathy are the two most important values my father has always tried to instil in us. Maybe the way he expressed his feelings was wrong, but whatever he said was for our betterment and good. I am glad he did so because with all the opportunities he has provided me, I believe there is nothing I cannot do as a girl—travelling, achieving things, or making life-changing decisions. And it's all thanks to him."*

The courage to have difficult conversations is the lifeblood of every single relationship. This simple way of initiating a conversation opened the gates for something much more meaningful that helped me to revive my relationship with my father to a large extent.

The reality of our society is not simply black or white but all shades of grey. I have learned to care for my father. Being the eldest among siblings, I try to be a good sister and a better human being every day, aiming to end this generational trauma. I have learnt to embrace my past and take control of my narrative. It motivates me to focus my energy on growth, exploration, and leading my life with courageous empathy.

# 13

# *Mindfulness at the Workplace: an experiential learning*

It was the end of 2004. I just completed my bachelor's in Marine Engineering and was called by my company office in Mumbai to complete official formalities before joining the MSC-owned ship *MV Teresa*. The Port of joining was Singapore.

The second engineer, Anirban Saha was also joining the same ship. Together we boarded the Air India flight from Mumbai. Mr. Saha freed me of all the fears and hassles that could have beset a first-time traveller abroad, who, at the age of 22, was starting a professional career as a Fifth engineer on board.

The hopping flight via Hyderabad took us 9 hours to reach Singapore's Changi airport at around 10 a.m. local time. The agent who had come to receive us ferried us to our hotel, about

30 minutes from the airport. Our ship was expected to arrive in Singapore sometime that night. We both had been awake practically throughout the journey and were exhausted. After an early dinner, we rested till the shipping agent came, around midnight, to drive us to the port where *MV Teresa* was in the process of getting anchored.

She was a container carrier and had already sailed for 32 years, which is considered a long time for a ship to survive at sea. With a length of 265 meters, the ship had a maximum capacity of carrying 6200 containers of standard sizes (TEU).

At two a.m., we made our way onto the ship via the lowered gangway and were promptly escorted to the captain's office to complete the signing-in formalities. Captain J. Fernandes was a tall, handsome guy, in his mid-40s with a grave yet endearing personality. As I would come to know eventually, he was loved by everyone on the ship for his caring nature. We were asked to report to the engine room immediately. I stowed my little luggage in my cabin, donned a boiler suit and industrial boots, and joined Mr. Saha as we made our way to the engine room.

Contrary to its name, a ship's engine room is not just one room. It is a vast space situated in the aft portion of the ship. Spread over many floors, it accommodates not only the ship's main engine but also all other supporting machinery required to run an ocean-going ship. You can call it the engineers' den, the main working place for all engineers on board. Whoever we met greeted us with a welcome gesture. Especially happy was Santosh, the Fourth engineer. Till now, there was no Fifth engineer on the ship. So, he got the satisfaction of having at least one engineer junior to him. He was busy taking the crude oil supply—the fuel for the main engine. The starboard ship's side door was kept open to receive the oil through pipelines from the filling boats. My immediate job was to assist Santosh.

During my training, I've had the opportunity to visit various ships and their engine rooms while docked. But this was something different. It was not just some casual watching; *I owned the responsibility for every action now.* Santosh explained all the details—various oil pipelines, related valves, and their connection to different reservoir tanks in the ship. Over time, I would be responsible for monitoring the ship's oil reserves and sending reports in advance to appropriate ports for replenishment.

The ship had 24 crews—twelve on the engine side, ten navigation crews, and a chief cook and steward. The Chief Engineer and Chief Officer were from Ukraine; the chief cook was from Colombo—the rest were from India. As the day proceeded, Santosh became a sort of elder brother to me. He hailed from Goa. In fact, almost half of the crew, including Captain Fernandes, belonged to Goa.

Work continued throughout the day with intermittent intervals for breakfast, lunch and other short breaks. I returned to my cabin in the evening to fall asleep almost instantly after a bath and a quick dinner. Loading and unloading continued on the ship. In the middle of the night, I was awoken by the gentle rocking of my bed. It took me a moment to realise that the ship had set sail for her next destination, Jakarta. The ship was plying on a long route covering most of the Indian Ocean, from the farthest east to the most distant west. Its regular course was Singapore, Jakarta, Freemantle in Australia before turning westward and heading further south to touch some ports near the Tropic of Capricorn in the African continent.

My work hours were scheduled to be 8 a.m. – 6 p.m. every day. Other engineers worked in two shifts of 4 hours each with an additional overtime working slot of 2 hours. However, in an emergency, all engine crew had to be present together.

By 8 a.m., I was at my workplace the following day. This was my first experience of being in the engine room with its main engines running. The sound of all the machines was deafening; ear muffs and helmets were a must. Despite the vast ventilation system with all-around networks of exhaust and fresh air inlet ducts, the engine room temperature was likely over 40 degrees Celsius with high humidity, especially since the ship was navigating in a tropical region. The only intermittent comfort was in the engine control room, which was air-conditioned.

Unlike modern Unmanned Machinery Space (UMS) ships, the *MV Teresa* required a manual round-the-clock watch. With two propellers powered by two main engines, the visible part of which was spread over four floors, with a total of 96000 horsepower, the maintenance of the main engines, along with a vast amount of machinery on the ship, could be expected to be challenging though a self-satisfying task.

Usually, I would utilise the two designated tea breaks of twenty minutes each, one at 11 a.m. and the other at 4 p.m., to climb up to the main deck to find some suitable spot to watch the ocean without any gears or pipelines obstructing my view. From my vantage point, the ship, moving at an average speed of 21 nautical miles per hour, sailed royally, cutting through the water like an arrow, creating a 'V-shaped' pattern of waves on either side. As far as one could see, there was water all around, giving the impression that the earth was a spherical ball of seawater with our ship positioned on top of it.

Three days passed before I could manage time to call home using the satellite phone on the navigation deck. Charges were 3 US dollars a minute, which would be deducted from my salary. Being conscious of the high call charges, I had written down a short and precise message to speak on the phone. True to my plan, I finished the call in less than a minute.

The next day, over breakfast, Captain Fernandes genially asked me, "Prem, what *did* you talk about in less than a minute?"

And whomever I met asked me the same question that day. I realised that practically everyone on the ship knew and was amused by my short phone call. It felt good being a part of this community where such a small act could become a means of striking up conversations and relationships.

The ship kept sailing with occasional stops at different ports. Each port visit lasted around 24 hours, a little more or less, depending on the loading and unloading of containers. This would be the only time when the main engines would be off, which meant that most supporting machines would either be stopped or run at reduced capacity, thus relieving all the engineers to some extent. Following a brief stay in Jakarta, our ship set sail for her next destination, Freemantle in Australia.

With a limited crew, the work pressure on board was always tremendous. I resumed the morning and evening meditation sessions I had practised since college. It kept me emotionally strong to cope with the new life at sea, where we sometimes went days without touching land.

After four days, the ship arrived at Freemantle port. While I was working in the engine room at Freemantle, I got a call from the captain, who asked me to urgently come to my cabin. Not sure what to expect, I was a little tensed, as during the last surprise inspection captain advised me to keep my room clean. Quickly I made my way to my cabin where I found Captain Fernandes standing alongside two Australian immigration officers.

Before I got even more panicked, the senior immigration officer said he wanted to teach the other guy, a young and new joiner, how to carry out a formal search operation in case it was required.

I had only one trolley bag that also had only a few contents. The senior officer frisked through my belongings, seemingly *dissatisfied* with nothing much to search for. In particular, his attention was drawn by the few books I carried on yoga and meditation.

"Are you a *preacher*?" asked the senior official while still examining my belongings and explaining the search process to the younger officer.

"Well, I think I am a follower rather than a preacher," was my spontaneous response. Until then, I never considered myself a teacher of meditation or yoga. It was not until years later that I realised the prescient nature of the words spoken by the immigration officer. After a brief inspection, both officials left. Captain looked satisfied with the cleanliness of my room, though he didn't comment on it.

Following a brief stopover at Freemantle, the ship sailed towards her next destination—Port Louis in Mauritius. Reaching there would take us around eight days and eight nights of nonstop sailing.

Just after leaving Freemantle, one day, we had a mock 'Abandon Ship and Fire' drill. Except for the two persons in the engine room and two on the navigation deck, everyone on the ship, including the cook and steward, assembled at the muster station, wearing boiler suits and life jackets. This was one of the rare moments when nearly all the crew gathered together. The Second officer facilitated the drill, explaining in detail the lowering mechanism of the lifeboat when, in case of some extreme emergency, abandoning the ship was the only option left.

*This taught me that nothing can be taken lightly when it comes to the safety of the workplace and its contents, which, in this case, was the ship and her cargo. However, the priority of saving lives stands superior to all.*

## The duality of time

One day I came across a note on the engine control room noticeboard—'*Retard* clock by 1 hour today'. Not knowing its significance, I asked Santosh about it. "As we are moving west", he explained, "We are gaining time. So, to match the local time, it is the general practice to adjust the ship's clocks at night, after every few days, and sometimes every other day also, as required. It means the night will be 1 hour longer for us today. Nonetheless, daytime working hours remain unchanged."

I was happy at the prospect of getting 1 hour of extra sleep that night and subsequently on each night whenever the clock will be retarded. However, Santosh and Third Engineer Khan Saab both had a smirk on their faces.

"*Panch saab*[*]," Khan Saab said, "just keep in mind that on the return journey, our clock will be set forward, and you will have shorter nights to sleep."

*I understood the nature of duality, which is conspicuous by its presence in this world. Happiness and distress are two faces of the same coin. I needed to learn to tolerate both.*

A scheduled inspection of our ship at Durban by the South African Maritime Safety Association (SAMSA) was coming up shortly. After the inspection by AMSA, Australian Maritime Safety Association, in Freemantle, I was relieved that the extra workload was over. However, with SAMSA on the horizon, I knew that another round of extra work awaited the crew. To

* A casual way to address a fifth engineer on board.

accommodate this workload, my watch was reset from 6 a.m. to 6 p.m.

Seeing me a bit annoyed, Motorman Ali spoke, "*Main bhi aisa hi sochata tha Paanch Saab, par jahaj pe kaam kabhi khatam nahin hota.*" Then, after a moment of reflection, he offered me a solution, "*Man ko mana lo, sab thik ho jayega.*" (I, too, used to think like that, but sir, the work on a ship never truly ends. Make up your mind and, everything eventually will fall into place).

It dawned on me that every workplace has its own unique needs and demands—*The solution was to develop acceptance and a positive mindset towards the work.*

On the first night itself, I got confused with the retarded clock, and instead of 6 a.m., the next morning, I arrived at 7 in the engine room. Khan Saab inquired about my tardiness, but before I could even respond, he picked up on my confusion. With a quick glance at the control room clock, I realised my mistake. Without missing a beat, Khan Saab reassured me, "*Paanch Saab, dariya sab ko dhoka deti hai* (the ocean confuses even an experienced person)," and chuckled, "Sometimes I *myself* get confused by the clock even after spending so many years in the sea." He was someone who didn't mind such a thing as long as one was sincere and committed to the duty.

## Deck party

En route to Mauritius, one day, we had a night party on the main deck of the moving ship, featuring a variety of food and an open-air barbeque. Amidst the moonlight flooding us, the stars shone brightly, and the rhythmic sound of the ocean waves echoed in the air, creating a serene ambience. As a vegetarian, my options for food were limited, still, I eagerly anticipated the deck party as it was an opportunity to spend quality time with most of the crew.

Leaving behind the engineer on watch, Motorman Jacob also came to have his dinner. Finding Mr. Saha sitting in a pensive mood alone in a corner, Jacob filled up his plate and chose to sit beside him for company. I recalled hearing from Ramnath, the fireman, about a motorman who had committed suicide in his room a few days before my joining. "He was a good friend of mine," Ramnath had told me, "And I could *never* guess that he would do anything like this. We had to make an emergency stop at the nearest port to send his dead body to India." After that incident, the Captain encouraged everyone to talk and spend time together.

*I realised that even though we worked with machines, we ourselves were not machines. We possess emotions. Anyone can go through a low phase in their life. We need to be mindful of talking to people around us. We may not know how even one small quality interaction with someone can drastically change the course of a person's life.*

After a few more days of sailing, we berthed at Port Loius, where an unforgettable incident occurred. At the end of a full day of work, I returned to my cabin, bathed, but somehow didn't have any desire to go for dinner. While lying on the bed,

I frisked through some of the books I carried and fell into a deep sleep.

About two hours later, my doorbell rang. With the intercom not working, the only time someone would ring my doorbell would be to announce some emergency call from the engine room. I opened the door sleepily, expecting to be called on duty. To my relief, I found Stephen, the young Steward, standing there.

"Did you have dinner?" he asked.

"*No*. I slept," I mumbled. Later, I learned that Stephen had waited for me in the dining hall, and realising that my vegetarian meal would get over, he had filled a plate and put a wrapper around it. He informed the Captain of my absence, who told him to contact me in person.

Discomfited, I went to the mess quickly. It was already very late. Everyone had taken their dinner. Stephen stayed with me all through till I finished eating. I fell short of words to express my gratitude to him. From that day on, even if I wanted to skip a meal for some reason, I would make sure to go just for Stephen—it was like a fear based on love.

*This incident taught me to appreciate small gestures of concern. I learnt to be mindful of the people around me. Sometimes, even a small act of kindness and consideration can mean a lot to the other person.*

I slept after dinner, not realising that a wonderful surprise was awaiting me. Around midnight the doorbell rang again. Again I opened the door half-asleep, thinking some emergency had arisen. To my utmost surprise, I found Abhishek, my batchmate, at the door. His ship also happened to be in Port Louis. Apparently, the captains of both vessels had conversed about their crew, and realising that Abhishek and I were batchmates, Abhishek was released from his watch to come and meet me.

Just a few months back, we had a farewell ceremony at college. We never expected to meet again so soon, and that too in such a remote place in the world. In a short time, we asked each other many questions about our first sailing experiences. Then Abhishek had to take his leave, for he was on the night watch in the engine room. I accompanied him till gangway. As he left, I was left to wonder: Among hundreds of thousands of ports worldwide, what is the possibility of meeting someone like this? Did this happen by *chance*, or is there a plan behind everything?

The next day Captain Fernandes asked me whether I could meet my batchmate the previous night. I thanked Captain for being kind to arrange this, knowing it was not part of his job in any way.

*I realised these extra details in caring for subordinates make working life less stressful and keep aids attached, gaining their loyalty. The feeling of caring surpasses duty.*

Our next stop was Durban. It was the farthest west in our route, after which, on the return journey, the ship halted at Le Port, a small port city in Réunion Island—a French department in the Indian Ocean.

The next day after leaving Le port, in the evening, as I was going around the machinery, noting their running parameters,

I noticed the exhaust temperature of the sixth cylinder of the port-side engine rising. From its usual reading of 340 degrees Celsius, the needle went on to read 360, 370, and 390 and crossed 400 in front of my eyes. The engine was constantly gaining more speed with an unusually loud noise. Even before I could report to the engine control room, the other Third engineer on watch, Mr. Silva, reached the spot. Some quick decisions had to be taken. These are moments when the quickness and expertise of engineers on board can be seen in action. The first priority was to protect the engine somehow. In swift consultation with Mr. Saha, Silva turned both main engines off.

*I learnt that when a system goes out of control and if you cannot find out the cause for it at the first instance, don't panic. Just turn the system off like we did with the main engine. Having taken the first and most important step for protection, start investigating for probable causes.*

Immediately there was a call from the duty officer on the bridge who wanted to know *why* we turned off the engines. Mr. Silva informed him about the situation at hand. Captain Fernandes was in the engine room even before the phone was kept down. Remaining stagnant like this in the middle of the ocean meant a loss to the company and a risk to the ship too.

Mr. Silva suspected a scavenge fire. It was decided to check the under-piston spaces of the port side engine just in case there was any sludge accumulation. With all the blowers running inside the main engine, it would take *at least* two hours before the engine could be cooled down sufficiently to allow us to open and inspect the scavenge spaces safely. In the meantime, the engine crew took turns having dinner to prepare for the next operation.

Ramnath secretly spoke in my ears, "The sixth cylinder has the sludge accumulation."

"What makes you so *certain*?" I asked.

"Because," he replied, "I cleaned the scavenge spaces last time but, due to time constraints, left the last cylinder half-clean."

Of course, these secrets were supposed to be kept from the senior engineers.

As suspected by Ramnath, the last unit had a good amount of sludge accumulation, which apparently caught fire. With almost all the engine crew working together, the cleaning of under-piston spaces of all the units and reassembling the whole system went on for more than 5 hours. A little past midnight, the main engines were successfully restarted. For everyone, it was a feeling of triumph.

*I learned the lesson—even though it may be hectic, teamwork with a goal makes working life a satisfying experience.*

## An adventure and a life-changing experience

Our voyage continued, and after a week, we found ourselves back in Singapore. It would take us nearly 40 days to complete the ring route, which we started from Singapore. After a brief stay there, the ship set sail for Jakarta.

A day after leaving Jakarta, we kept getting information about a ship '*MV Denisse*' that had sent out an SOS signal. The ship was sinking in the middle of the ocean, a little ahead of our route towards Freemantle. During lunch also, I found the crew discussing this. After a quick lunch, I returned to the engine room only to discover that I was relieved from my watch as a team of four members, comprising of me, motorman Ali, welder Joseph, and fireman Ramnath, had been tasked with providing assistance to the sinking vessel.

Captain Fernandes explained that *MV Denisse* was a container carrier that had got its engine room flooded, apparently due to a rupture in some seawater pipeline. The exact reason would be clear only when the ship reached a dry dock. The watertight doors segregating the engine room compartment from the rest of the ship worked perfectly, and as of now, the ship's condition was stable. However, the ship needed help with drinking water and other manual jobs to restore her condition to the extent that she could be towed to the dry dock at the nearest port.

Despite being the youngest in the team, I was made in charge of the group. However, this didn't matter much since everyone else in my team was as inexperienced as me when it came to aiding a ship in distress out in the middle of the ocean. A situation like this is rare, and most mariners never encounter such a circumstance in their entire sailing career, where they have to face a sinking ship either being personally present on board or being part of a rescue mission to assist another ship.

We were expected to be in the vicinity of *MV Denisse* sometime in the night. Until then, another ship was already assisting her with the rescue operation. We were supposed to take over from them.

At around 10 p.m., our ship slowed down and reached a standstill. Captain Fernandes made sure that we all had our life jackets on properly. As the darkness of night pervaded in all directions, I could spot a light in the middle of the ocean, likely 5–6 nautical miles away. That was our destination, *MV Denisse*.

A tug boat, which had arrived from the nearest port, was already there to ferry us to *MV Denisse*. A small group of the crew assembled on deck as they saw four of us using the rope ladder to climb down several meters from the main deck to the flatbed of the tug boat. With the help of the ship's provision crane, we also lowered several cans of potable water. As the tug boat ferried us close to *MV Denisse*, we could see the ship in a tilted condition, with the aft portion barely a few feet above the water level, giving the front part of the ship the appearance of being flung. With containers stacked high on deck, the ship's stability seemed precarious. However, a sense of duty was overpowering; none of us feared anything.

The ship had its seaside door open to let us in directly from the boat. The Captain of the ship was standing there to guide us. Using the provision crane on the ship, the water cans were lifted, and then Joseph stepped inside first, keeping a foot on the ridge of the boat and then taking a jump to put his next foot on the little raised platform of the ship's floor, inside the open door. Then Ali and Ramnath entered the ship the same way.

I was the last in the cue.

As soon as I kept my left foot on the ridge of the boat, a sudden massive wave caused the protective rubber tyres in front of the boat to squeeze out the space between the tyres and the vertical ridge where I had placed my leg. The pressure was so intense that I couldn't even consider trying to get free. It felt as if vertical walls with massive force were pressing into my left leg from all sides. As a natural biological response, I shouted as loud as I could, in complete helplessness. Never in my entire life had I felt such tremendous pain.

With the squeezed rubber tyre still jamming my leg, I knew my leg would turn into pulp in seconds. I kept yelling. Fortunately, the tugboat pilot understood the urgency of the situation and promptly pulled the boat backwards, releasing my leg from the grip of the tyre.

In excruciating pain, I stumbled towards the inner side of the tug, crashing on the floor helplessly. After a minute or so, I somehow got up and waved at my mates standing on the other side, who evidently were worried about my safety.

I waited for the waves to subside a bit before I could make another attempt to enter the ship. I signalled the pilot to move the tug closer. With much difficulty, I put my right leg on the ridge, this time keeping a close eye on the tyres in front. I was determined to make it this time, no matter what. As I took a leap using only the right leg effectively, I found myself inside the ship.

To some extent, my fellow crew were relieved to see me inside, though I was in no condition to stand on my own. I felt bad to add to the ongoing chaos, but it couldn't be helped. My team members carried me inside the dishevelled dining hall of the ship and seated me in a chair before leaving for their assigned work.

As time went by, my left leg started swelling. I became a centre of sympathy for the crew on board *MV Denisse*, mostly Indians, who frequented the dining hall to have whatever food was available. They looked fatigued, physically and mentally both. How much longer they would have to be there like this was still uncertain. Through my conversations with them, I gathered that after the engine room flooding was detected on *MV Denisse*, everyone was instructed to assemble at the muster station. A real abandon ship drill was anticipated to be carried out in case the watertight door segregating the engine room from the rest of the ship did not work efficiently.

As the ship slowly kept sinking and tilting at the back, the port side lifeboat was tried to be lowered, but to everyone's utmost *shock*, as is common in many such cases, the lifeboat lowering mechanism failed, leaving everyone in a panic beyond imagination. Thankfully, the spare lifeboat on the starboard side was tested, and its lowering mechanism was found to be working perfectly. Everyone waited for a signal from the captain about the next move.

The crew got divided in their opinions. Some wanted to leave using the lifeboat, while others wanted to stay on board and wait for the next command from the captain. *Fortunately*, after five hours, the ship ceased to sink any further. The watertight doors were found to work perfectly.

*When in the midst of the ocean, chances of survival are always more aboard a larger ship rather than a mere lifeboat. Hence, only when it is absolutely certain that the ship is going to sink should abandoning it become an option.*

After four hours of work, my team members returned. I told them I could not go back to the tug through sea side doors. Consequently, a stretcher was used to lower me down from the ship's provision crane onto the tug boat. By this time, the sun was already on the horizon. The warmth of sunlight felt comfortable as I lay on the stretcher. As the boat advanced forward, my team members guarded me against the salty sea water splashes. As I neared *MV Teresa*, I felt like coming home where everything would be taken care of. News of my accident had already reached the ship. Many assembled on deck, including Captain Fernandes, as everyone witnessed a deck crew lifting me, laying on the stretcher, up from the boat using the crane.

Chief Officer Volodymyr did first aid by skilfully wrapping cotton and bamboo sticks around my left leg.

"It is a fracture," he spoke confidently, looking at the amount of swelling, "Possibly even a double fracture."

I listened silently, *not* believing his words.

Still on the stretcher, I was carried to my room. The Steward brought me lunch, and I couldn't help but feel like a helpless child. I felt grateful for everyone's care and attention. Captain Fernandes decided I would see a doctor at our next destination,

Freemantle, which was 2 to 3 days away. However, soon after, the Captain and Chief Officer Volodymyr returned.

The Captain said, "Prem, delayed treatment may create blood clotting in your leg. So we have decided to relieve you at Christmas Island close by. Agents assigned by the shipping company will take care of your treatment." Official formalities were completed, and I signed-off. Our ship sailed for three hours to discharge me at Christmas Island, an Australian territory in the Indian Ocean, lying south of Java, Indonesia. The Island did not have a port for big ships. Again I was put on a stretcher and, along with my luggage, using the provision crane, I was lowered on a tug boat which would take me to the jetty nearby.

Many crews assembled on deck as I bid a last goodbye to them. Probably, my contact with them was allotted only for this amount of time. I would ever remain indebted to all of them for their camaraderie. I gave a last look at the ship *MV Teresa*, which I boarded in Singapore 48 days ago. I told Santosh to be in touch through emails.

The waiting ambulance at the jetty carried me to the only hospital on the island. With a population of just two thousand, the Island appeared to be an idyllic countryside with a range of low and high mountains.

"*It's a big one*," the nurse exclaimed after showing me the X-ray plate.

Even I could clearly figure out the complete fracture in the left leg's tibia, the main bone. The bone looked like a log of dry wood broken down in its middle. I could not believe how I could jump from the tug boat inside the *MV Denisse* with this injured leg. The words of Chief Officer Volodymyr proved to be prophetic.

*I realised there is no match to the experience of a senior person.*

An all-around plaster was cast from the knee to the toe of my left leg. Dr. Seeback, who was treating me, decided to send me to Perth in mainland Australia for surgery, as the Island lacked such a facility. Soon, the arrangements were made, and I was transported to Perth via a regular fan-propelled aircraft, where I was admitted to St John of God Hospital. As I would come to know, it was one of the finest hospitals in Western Australia.

The following day the operation was done using a central nailing process. Opening my knee, a rod was inserted through the central axis of the tibia. The day after the operation, a physiotherapist encouraged me to get out of bed and taught me how to walk with a crutch. I had to train my left leg to take the pressure as comfortably as I could at this stage. It felt as if I was starting from scratch, like a toddler learning to walk. The therapy session continued every day.

The entire care system left me in awe. Everywhere things were arranged smoothly without me going through the least of hassles. MSC office in Perth had not only taken responsibility for the financial aspects of treatment but also assigned Robert Black, a young officer in his mid-twenties, to take care of me in case I needed any additional help.

To my delight, three days later, Santosh and Joseph came to visit me in the hospital. After I saw them last at Christmas Island, they were unaware of my subsequent whereabouts. Eventually, *MV Teresa* sailed to Freemantle, a port city adjacent to Perth. When Santosh was on shore leave, someone at the Seafarers Club informed him about me.

I showed my X-ray plate to Joseph. He was there at *MV Denisse* when, in this condition, I had attempted a jump from the tug boat to the inside of the ship without realising that it could be such a severe fracture.

Joseph's mouth was agape in disbelief upon gazing at the X-ray plate.

"*Had* I known this," I said, "I definitely would not have made that move." Before leaving, Santosh snapped a group photo, which he planned to share with all the crew on board.

Noticing that I was having a difficult time finding food that suited my Indian palate, Robert, my company officer, suggested that I shift to the Seafarers Club, where I could manage to get some Indian cuisine. I could visit Dr. Skinner for a check-up after one week or so.

I agreed.

Seafarers Club was a familiar place for me, having visited this place while on shore leave during my last trip to Freemantle. It had some guest rooms, a prayer hall, a well-maintained kitchen, an internet café, and a common items shop catering to the needs of seafarers. I was given the liberty to access the Club's kitchen, where I would manage to prepare a daily meal of rice with either vegetables or *dal*.

I kept up with my self-physiotherapy sessions and continued practising walking with crutches. I resumed my regular meditation routine, which had been discontinued since the accident. In the afternoons, I spent time with the local kids who came to the club to play. While at the Seafarers Club, I searched the internet for the address of Hare Krishna temple and found it was in Bayswater, around 30 km from the Club.

Robert talked at the Club, and the next day after breakfast, Patrick, one of the volunteers at the Club, offered to drop me at Bayswater. He planned to fetch someone from Perth Airport. Bayswater happened to be en route.

Things had drastically changed for me over the past two weeks. *It was uncertain how long it would take me to recover completely*—it could be months. I was visiting the temple to seek some solace. I had decided to wait until I returned to India to inform my parents to prevent them from worrying unnecessarily.

The day was bright and sunny as I sat next to Patrick in the passenger's seat. The car glided smoothly along the road, flanked by rows of tall, beautiful trees on both sides. Patrick turned on the radio in the car. The station was playing pop songs, the lyrics of which I could not make out much, with the track changing every few minutes. We were expected to be at Bayswater in around half an hour or so.

Leaving behind relatively busy city roads, the car eventually pulled into a sparsely populated suburb. As the radio station played the next song, I found myself drawn to the guitar notes, which sounded familiar. To my surprise and delight, it was one of my favourite tunes—'*My Sweet Lord*' by George Harrison. It was George's most successful hit single from his album *All Things Must Pass,* released more than four decades ago.

George's heartfelt lyrics echoed:
'*My sweet Lord.*
*I really want to see you,*
*I really want to be with you,*
*but it takes so long, my Lord.*'

And my eyes moistened. I struggled to conceal my tears. Out of all the songs in this world, what made the radio station play this particular tune that perfectly reflected my feelings?

The song also featured the recurring divine refrain of '*Hallelujah*' intertwined with the chants of '*Hare Krishna*' and '*Hare Rama*'. I couldn't help but wonder whether this was a mere coincidence or if there is one *Supreme* who has a plan for me.

The song provided me with the comfort I was seeking as if it was whispering, 'Don't *fret*; everything will turn out all right for you.'

A little later, after the song was over, I reached the temple. It was situated in a low-density residential suburb. Patrick was supposed to pick me up on his way back from the airport in about an hour.

As I entered inside, I found a lady volunteer, absorbed in herself, melodiously chanting the complete 'Hare Krishna

Hare Rama' mantra, though in a different melody, on a harmonium:

*Hare Krishna Hare Krishna*
*Krishna Krishna Hare Hare*
*Hare Rama Hare Rama*
*Rama Rama Hare Hare*

I sat on the floor, immersing myself, listening to the divine sound vibration while beholding the beautiful form of Radha Krishna on the altar. The uncertainty I had been grappling with about my future dissipated entirely.

Two days later, I visited Doctor Skinner, who wrote in my report, "I am happy to see Prem improving fast." He permitted me to fly back to India any time after that. The following night I departed for Mumbai.

Sometimes there is a once-in-a-lifetime experience that changes the way you look at the world. My first 48 days outside India were one such experience. The lessons I learned then remained with me till today. Among all the people I came across so far, the ones on the ship were the least discriminatory. No one cared about where one came from or what colour, caste, creed, country, or religion they belonged to.

*I've come to understand that differences evaporate when we realise we need each other. We knew that among all the people in the world, those who would help us right now were the few of the crew members around us.*

It's important to stay mindful and keep our inner eyes open to everything that life teaches us. There are certain things that *you* decide in life, and then there are things that *life* decides for you. Be flexible to accept both. Looking back, I recall meeting my batchmate, Abhishek, last time in Mauritius almost two decades ago.

*It's easy to underestimate the impact that people have on our lives, but when they're no longer around, sometimes all we're left with is only cherished memories. Be mindful of your every interaction. From our words, actions, and intentions, we should not wish or do anything unbecoming to anyone we might regret later.*

# 14

## *Synergy*

While brushing my teeth one day, I observed that my utmost effort was unconsciously directed towards achieving a clean appearance of my front teeth—the visible part to others. This inclination may stem from the fact that cleaning the inner surfaces of teeth is comparatively more challenging and scarcely noticed by anyone but oneself.

I drew a parallel between this incident and our lives. It could be that a lot of endeavours are put into making shine that part of our personality visible to others. But what is more important is to develop our inner personality by cultivating those habits that foster our emotional and physical well-being. Acknowledge and effectively manage the subtle roles that three modes play in our lives with a specific emphasis on cultivating goodness while conscientiously keeping the effects of passion and ignorance to a minimum.

As outlined in this book, the mindfulness practices that help in this regard can be succinctly summarised into the following key points:

1. Practice mindful breathing and appropriate pranayam regularly, understanding that it helps achieve a balance between all types of life airs—a must for the proper functioning of our gross and subtle body.
2. Keep healthy recreation and sleep habits. Maintain a regulation in diet and consume an adequate quantity of water.
3. Apply SEC, 'scan – empathise – choose', to deal with your negative emotions. Doing it once a day will make you mindful of the emergence of negative emotions and prepare you to respond appropriately.
4. Listen to your physical body—do a mindful complete or partial body scan as and when required.
5. Be a carrier of positivity. Develop a meaningful and mindful perception of the world around you—be a honey bee, not a fly.
6. Strive to preserve the warmth of relationships. A meaningful relationship with someone is often the one thing that can bring the greatest happiness into your life.

Our mental and physical states are very much interlinked; thus, caring for both is vital to living holistically. All standard lifestyle practices aligned with the principles of the mode of goodness discussed so far work in synergy. Enhancing one aspect will positively affect other elements, whether directly or indirectly.

For instance, the nutritional value we derive from our meals is not solely determined by the nutrients in the food. It also depends on the amount of those nutrients that our body can assimilate and utilise effectively. This ability is influenced by our digestive power. In addition to other factors, our ability to digest food well also relies on having a stable state of mind. When the mind is tense, fearful, uncertain, or anxious, it can lead to the release of harmful chemicals in the body that interfere with the proper digestion and absorption of nutrients.

A fulfilling relationship leads to a happy mind. This contented state of mind ensures sound sleep. Good sleep, in turn, leads to a stable mind and healthy body. The opposite is equally true—an agitated mind causes disturbed sleep, which in turn affects the person's health.

Thus, though all the elements of mindfulness—mindful eating, mindful speech, mindfulness in our dealings, mindful breathing or pranayam, meditation, etc. may appear to be separate stand-alone practices, their effects are significantly interlinked. When practised together, all these elements work in synergy, resulting in a happy and healthy individual in whom all negative emotions, including *deep-rooted* ones, disappear.

Enrich your life with the elements of goodness, and then inspire a few others to do the same. Each day, take a moment to consider how you can contribute to making the world a better place. Let's spread joy and positivity wherever we go, serving as ambassadors of kindness. By sharing knowledge and connecting people to a life of goodness, we can create a ripple effect of positive change in the world around us.

*****

---

I greatly appreciate the time you took to read my book, and I hope you enjoyed it. Your honest review or rating on Amazon would mean the world to me. It helps the book reach a wider audience, and I genuinely look forward to hearing about your experience.

Prem Gopal Das
premgopal@vedantayogashala.in

Also by **Prem Gopal Das**

## Success Hacks for Teens:

### *30 Prompts and Practices to Enhance Well-being and Productivity*

If you enjoyed this book, don't miss **Success Hacks for Teens** — packed with practical tips, guided prompts, and easy-to-use tools to help you stay balanced and focused in every area of life.

Inside, you'll find universal principles you can put into practice as a teen — or, if you're an adult, you might think, "No one told me this when I was a teen."

**Available on Amazon**
*Scan the QR code or visit:*
www.amazon.com/dp/B0FD7FBW5R

# *Acknowledgements*

I am deeply grateful to all my friends, who, with their encouragement and camaraderie, helped me realise the production of this book from its inception to its completion. I want to extend a special thanks to everyone who has graciously allowed me to share their stories within the pages of this book; their names will be revealed as you read on.

I would also like to express my heartfelt appreciation to Elina Majumdar for her invaluable contribution to the copy editing of the book, Rajesh Thakkar for the typesetting and book layout, P. Markovic for impressive cover design and Amit for being instrumental in analysing and developing the beta version of the book.

I am very much grateful to Dr Prabhakar Singh, an Ayurveda expert, from whom - over the years - I have learned vital principles of maintaining a healthy lifestyle. I would also like to thank Dr Kusagradhi Ghose, Samar Mallick, Krishna, Vikram, and Nitin, who played crucial roles in various stages of the book's production.

Finally, I want to thank you for reading this book. I sincerely hope the principles discussed here will benefit you greatly.

# *About the Author*

Prem Gopal Das, born in 1982, has been a practitioner and teacher of meditative yoga and mindfulness practices for over two decades. His journey to the inner quest started young when he was still a higher secondary student. After completing his master's degree from *IIT Kharagpur*, he briefly worked in his professional career before becoming a full-time monk in 2008. Since then, he has been actively involved with offering courses, guidance, and counselling services to children, young adults, and families, with the aim of promoting a healthy and well-rounded lifestyle.

www.ingramcontent.com/pod-product-compliance
Ingram Content Group UK Ltd.
Pitfield, Milton Keynes, MK11 3LW, UK
UKHW021402190726
13845UKWH00028B/824

9 788196 566531